NEWCASTLE

DARK TALES
OF OLD
NEWCASTLE

Written and illustrated by

Pamela Armstrong

Bridge Studios
Northumberland
1990

Dedicated to my parents
Joyce and Colin

Thanks to Mr Stan Garbutt and
Mrs Margaret Barratt

All royalties donated to the MacMillan
Fund for Cancer Relief

First published in Great Britain in 1990

by Bridge Studios,
   Kirklands,
   The Old Vicarage,
   Scremerston,
   Berwick upon Tweed,
   Northumberland TD15 2RB.
   Tel.: 0289 302658/330274

© Pamela Armstrong

ISBN 1 872010 30 X

Typeset by EMS Phototypesetting,
Hide Hill, Berwick upon Tweed.

Printed in Great Britain by
Martin's of Berwick Ltd.

Contents

Chapter One

THE SHADOW OF
THE SCAFFOLD

To enter the Courtroom of Newcastle's Guildhall is to be transported back to the days when this was the town's principal court (1658-1885). The magnificent Jacobean hall with its hammerbeam room cannot fail to impress the visitor. Beyond the witness stand you can still see the benches where the judge and counsel sat – defence to the right of the judge, and prosecution to his left. However none of this splendour can disguise the fact that until the first quarter of the nineteenth century, Newcastle justice was rough justice.

Indeed, this architectural finery was merely a veneer to mask the often corrupt authority within.

THE BEST LAW AND ORDER

MONEY CAN BUY

Just as powerful interest groups held sway throughout the country as a whole, so from the reign of Elizabeth until 1835, the Newcastle Corporation was dominated by a coal trade power-block known as 'hostmen'. Far from wishing to break the grip of these rich merchants, successive monarchs (eager for coal trade tax revenue) merely confirmed their power. Predictably, this power extended to legal matters also. Local magisterial lists consistently reflect the dominance of a handful of leading coal trade families.

Rather than rely upon the objective rule of law, the use of friends, connections and even direct bribes, were all accepted ways of influencing a judge or magistrate throughout the length and breadth of Britain. Newcastle was governed by the coal trade for the coal trade, and magistrates mainly functioned to protect vested interests from interruption or irritation. Bribery and corruption were equally rife among the circuit judges dispatched north to uphold Royal Justice, and there were many irregularities too. It was traditional to keep a visiting judge well supplied with food and drink throughout a hearing, and such largesse must frequently have impeded a fair summing-up. Inebriate judges would have caused quite a stir, but few can have had the impact of the infamous Judge Jeffreys when he came to Newcastle on assize duty in August 1684. Jeffreys may not yet have earned the sobriquet of the 'Hanging Judge' but he nevertheless had a reputation to live down to on account of his bad temper and excessive drinking. One contemporary report describes his behaviour in Newcastle and relates the way in which he would sit:

drinking to filthy excess till two or three o'clock

in the morning, going to bed as drunk as a beast, and rising again with the symptoms of one who has drunk a cup too much

Jeffreys drank heavily during court sittings, but if he was not quite as sober as a judge ought to be, he nevertheless meant business when it came to hounding out the King's enemies:

instead of the gravity of the tribunal, the Judge with his railleries and his jests then acted the part of a harlequin. In his hand he held out a paper, telling the court in a menacing manner he had there got a black list of damned fannattiques, and was resolved to scour them

Few could have relished the prospect of facing trial under the dreaded Jeffreys, but if the men charged with upholding Royal Justice left much to be desired, those paid to police the streets also commanded scant respect.

The Elizabethan Town Council had little faith in their own soldiery, for in the Common Council entry for 1594 mention is made of a sum of money paid to certain sergeants:

For that they shoulde take no rewardes

By the eighteenth century, the ancient burgher

watch system was proving inadequate to meet the needs and pressures of a growing population and 1763 saw the founding of the Town Guard. Assembly point for the Guard was the Porch of St Nicholas Church whence, at 10 p.m. they would begin their nightly patrol, each patrol lasting until 6 a.m. next morning. Easily recognised by their greatcoats and lanterns, their duties included calling the time every half hour. Pay was half a guinea per week plus a full guinea at the end of each season. Courage was required to venture into the rat-infested 'chares' or lanes of some of the less savoury parts of town, but a shilling bonus per arrest offered some incentive and led, on occasion, to members of the Guard being over-zealous in the execution of their duty. Apart from this eighteenth century neighbourhood watch scheme, in times of crisis, troops of voluntary militia were raised, although frequent in-fighting often caused more problems than those they were called upon to solve. Newcastle did not, in fact, have a regular police force until 1836 – an earlier attempt in 1832 failing owing to outraged ratepayers objecting to the cost.

THE CONDEMNED

So much for the forces of law and order but what of the accused? In the courtroom of the Guildhall can still be seen the prisoner's box topped with inward turning spikes and fitted with shackles. Standing there evokes images of former prisoners nervously awaiting the final verdict. Not all would face the gallows however, and up until 1857, transportation was a common sentence especially for offences that hinted at an underlying social malaise.

Transportation

In 1790 Jane Stephenson was transported for seven years for stealing a gentleman's handkerchief. In these enlightened days we might feel that Jane was unfortunate; in fact by the standards of the time she was extremely lucky. The usual sentence for theft was the death penalty but in Jane's case this was commuted in an act of clemency. During the eighteenth century many a Newcastle prisoner would find himself hustled off to the Quayside and thrown into some dark ship's hold soon to be bound for Barbados or the Carolinas. Transportation was a popular legal solution for vagrancy and subversive activity, but as James I discovered, it was not always the solution it promised to be.

King James and the Reivers

The hills and dales of the Anglo-Scottish frontier were inhabited by a number of families who organised themselves in a tribal fashion. Known as 'reivers' they were a menace to administrations on both sides of the border. Sixteenth century mafiosi such as the Armstrongs, the Grahams and the Elliots, terrorised both farmer and traveller alike, and to venture from England to Scotland without a large armed escort would have been unthinkable. With the Union of the Crowns came the desire to remove this threat to stability once and for all. In 1606 King James concluded that wholesale transportation of offending families was the only solution, and the Graham family of Eskdale was singled out for immediate attention.

Seventy-two Grahams were rounded up and forcibly transported out of the Tyne under an armed guard, their destination Flushing in the Low Countries. The operation was completed without difficulty and the King was congratulated for his ingenious strategy. However removing the Grahams to Flushing was one matter, keeping them there was quite another. Subsequently the authorities seem to have overlooked the large influx of people with the unusual surname Maharg entering the Tyne. Apparently they were unaware that the Tyne

14

keelmen were assisting the Grahams to slip back into the country. In 1608 one:

Bold and desperate malefactor by the name of Graham

was hanged at Westgate for daring to return from transportation, but the overwhelming majority of Grahams escaped recapture and returned home to Eskdale, and as a glance at the Dumfries and Galloway telephone directory will demonstrate, they are still very numerous there to this day!

Corporal Punishment

Corporal punishment would have been a daily occurrence in the streets of the town. It may be difficult for us to appreciate the entertainment value of such spectacles, but our ancestors had no such qualms. They were hardened to death and pain, for after all they lived side by side with them in a way that we do not. Moreover with no television to soak up their cathartic drives and few being able to afford to buy their entertainment, these street spectacles provided a very popular diversion, especially the stocks, which offered potential for audience participation.

Offences meriting a stay in the stocks ranged from being drunk and disorderly, to using bad language in public. Petty offenders would be pelted with filth for hours before being thrown into the Tyne Bridge Tower to cool their heels. The stocks were set up in the market places and at the White Cross, and at the foot of the Fleshmarket where they no doubt provided a diversion for bored shoppers. For perpetual petty offenders, a little 'fustigation' or whipping tended to make the culprits think twice before misbehaving again.

In pre-Reformation days, the most Godly of citizens consented to being whipped through the streets as an act of penance. Centuries later, flagellation was used as a means to rid Newcastle of undesirables. In the wake of the Reformation, vagrancy arising from unemployment was endemic throughout the country. Large numbers of unofficial beggars trooped into town to the horror of the civic fathers who pointed out that no able-bodied person had the right to beg. Worse than begging was the fact that they were begetting children thus creating the beggars of the future. The mere threat of a public whipping was usually sufficient to persuade vagrants to move on to another town. Thus the authorities removed the problem from their own patch and pushed it on to someone else's instead.

If post-Reformation civic fathers took little action to deal with certain social problems, in matters of sin, action was swiftly taken.

In 1564 David Liddell, a Newcastle apprentice, was given forty-eight hours to leave the town for becoming too friendly with a Quayside servant lass. Had he remained on the third day, he would have been publicly whipped on the Sandhill – the traditional site for meting out punishment to fornicators. The girl did not escape so lightly. She was tarred and feathered, placed on a tumbril and then drawn backwards and forwards across the Sandhill. A placard describing her sins was hung about her neck so that all might know her guilt.

If further proof were needed that Elizabethan England was indeed a man's world, the 'branks' was kept in the Guildhall as a constant reminder. The branks was an iron muzzle used to punish women who forgot their place. A wife accused of nagging her husband could find herself clapped into it and dragged along the Sandhill on a lead. Should the branks prove ineffective there was always the ducking stool waiting nearby as a further deterrent.

Capital punishment always drew the best crowds and certain parts of town outside of the Walls were the most frequently used execution sites. This was not always the case however, and executions occasionally took place on the Sandhill. It is a pity that those splendid seventeenth

century houses with their overhanging galleries were not there on the 4th of May 1464, for they would have commanded a grandstand view of a very special event.

Beheadings and Blue Blooded Treason

On that day following the Battle of Hexham, no less than three Lordly Lancastrians were lead up a hastily erected scaffold and beheaded one by one. Lords Hungerford, Roos and Taillebois might well have felt aggrieved at their fate, for captured aristocrats were usually ransomed rather than executed. Scarcely a month previously this treacherous threesome had callously abandoned their colleague, Sir Ralph Percy, to a lonely death at the Battle of Hedgely Moor. Now it was their turn.

The sight of three Lords mounting the scaffold must have caused quite a stir, for only the blue-blooded could claim the privilege of being beheaded, this being both a swifter and less painful death than say hanging. Condemned aristocrats were usually conveyed to London to be dispatched on Tower Hill. Once justice had been seen to be done, the victims' heads were impaled on London Bridge and the limbs returned to their native region for display there. An early sixteenth century Common Council account records that 6*d* was:

Paide to ye heede man for putting y pinnacle
for hanging heedes

The limbs of commoners as well as those of
aristocrats were placed upon the old Tyne
Bridge, but it is the blue-blooded who stand out.
A multitude of notable limbs have included:

In 1305 the right arm of William Wallace; in
1306 the limbs of John Seton, equerry to the
Bruce; later that year the arms of Bruce's
younger Brothers; in 1323 the limbs of Andrew
de Harcla, in 1408 the limbs of Hotspur's father
the 4th Earl Percy; in 1415, the legs of Lord
Grey, and in 1461, an arm belonging to the Earl
of Wiltshire.

Both the Pilgrimage of Grace (1537) and the
Rising of the North (1569) originating among
the Catholic gentry of Northern England.
Ringleaders and vassals alike were hunted down
without mercy and in the wake of the sup-
pressions, the bridge parapet would have been
crowded with heads. These gruesome displays
may well have deterred the potentially seditious
but they would have constituted something of a
health hazard as the limbs of London executed
aristocrats would have reached Newcastle some
time after their owner's demise.

In spite of these public health drawbacks, Newcastle must have been an exciting place to be during the Anglo-Scottish Wars. The Scottish monarchs maintained a town house in the Bigg Market and there were frequent visits. One of the most satisfying was in September 1513 when a ship docked *en route* from Berwick to London bearing the embalmed corpse of James IV. James, together with the cream of Scotland's nobility died at Flodden in an abortive attempt to invade Northumberland. Ironically enough, less than ten years previously, the townspeople had turned out in their hundreds to give a rousing reception to James' bride to be, Princess Margaret – younger sister of Henry VIII. James was nearly thirty but the bride was less than twelve years of age.

Margaret had lodged in the Augustinian Friary which, after the Reformation, was dismantled by the Freemen of Newcastle who built an elegant block of almshouses instead. We now know this building as the Joicey Museum – and a marvellous museum it is, giving the visitor a vivid insight into the nature and development of old Newcastle. One of the most unusual aspects of the museum is that you can come face to face with the third Earl of Derwentwater, no mean feat when one considers that he was beheaded for high treason back in 1716!

The Derwentwater affair is too well known to need repetition here. Suffice to say that among the Derwentwater memorabilia can be seen the wax death mask taken within hours of his execution on Tower Hill. As the visitor gazes at the delicate, pallid features, the distance of the centuries falls away and we become all too aware of the human tragedy surrounding the 1715 Jacobite Rebellion in which the 26 year old Earl lost his life.

While beheading was reserved for the aristocracy, lesser mortals were launched into eternity using more mundane means. For much of its history, Newcastle was a garrison town. The military had its own way of dealing with offences and there are a number of records of execution by firing squad.

Firing Squad

Most of the recorded executions took place on the grounds of desertion, but on the 16th of May 1640, the Royalist leader Lord Conway shot a man in the Bigg Market on a charge of mutinous behaviour. Two culprits were rounded up and found to be equally guilty of inciting unrest, but Conway decided that to make an example of one of them would suffice. The two concerned were forced to draw lots in order to decide who would die. The loser was then shot without further ado and buried in St Andrew's Churchyard. If Conway's draconian actions were designed to instil backbone in his troops, they were singularly unsuccessful. During the Battle of Newburn, Conway's horsemen galloped away without firing a shot, their morale in tatters.

Without a doubt, Anthony Alexander could have taught Conway's men a great deal about coolness under fire. Anthony joined the army of George II and soon found himself in action at the 1745 Battle of Fontenoy. Despite displaying great courage and discipline, the English forces were routed by the French cavalry. Anthony was captured and he faced an uncertain future until the French commanders gave their English captives the option of 'taking the white cockade' – that is of joining the Franco-Scottish Jacobite Army then preparing to land in Scotland in support of Charles Edward Stuart. Anthony agreed to join them but it cannot have been an easy decision. To join the Jacobites would involve taking up arms against his fellow English soldiers. Capture would mean certain death.

Anthony enlisted in the Jacobite 'Fitzallen's Horse' and accepted French pay. He took part in the retreat from Derby, the victorious Battle of Falkirk and the bloodbath of Culloden. There he was captured along with the remnants of Fitzallen's Horsemen, and herded into a prison ship bound for Newcastle. Soldiers who had deserted the English flag for the Jacobite colours were soon identified and rounded up. Sad to relate, 23 year old Anthony's life of high adventure came to a sordid end at the hands of a firing squad on the Town Moor.

In the main, executions by firing squad were comparatively rare when compared to the numbers of people who died by hanging.

Hanging

Hanging was both cheap and efficient. It was a great favourite with authorities and populace alike. Tall and gaunt, the gallows nevertheless had a great appetite for human life. Mass hangings could be particularly cost effective. Captured 'reivers' or border raiders could expect no trial and no mercy. In 1532 thirty Armstrongs died together at the Westgate gallows and their heads were:

Caused to be set upon the Castell

In the eighteenth century the office of Town Hangman might not have been a particularly sought-after post but it was certainly a busy one here in Newcastle. The following are some of the more interesting hangings that took place on the Town Moor.

21st August 1752
Richard Brown (keelman) hanged for the murder of his daughter.

19th August 1754
Dorothy Catinby hanged for the murder of her illegitimate children.

7th August 1758
Alice Williamson (aged 68) hanged for burglary)

21st August 1776
Andrew McKenzie (soldier) hanged for highway robbery

21st August 1776
Robert Knowles (postman) hanged for opening letters and stealing from them.

(It will be noted that most of these executions followed the August assizes and that the last two represent a double hanging).

Newcastle Central Library possesses a fascinating collection of contemporary pamphlets and broadsheets. These pamphlets frequently give an account of the deceased's last hours. There is always a strong moralising element and drink, together with general loose living, are highlighted as key factors in the subject's downfall. Despite these general ingredients there is enough period detail to make them absorbing reading.

Public executions were regarded as little more than free entertainment and the town authorities considered them as opportunities for displaying civic pride. When Jane Jameson was executed for murder in 1829, the procession up to the Town Moor included the following:

> the Town sergeants on horseback with cocked hats and swords the town marshall also on horseback in his official costume; the cart with the prisoner sitting on her coffin, guarded on each side by eight free porters with javelins, and ten constables with their staves; then came the mourning coach containing the chaplain, the under sherrif, the gaoler and the clerk of St Andrews

After a procession like that, Jane's demise was surely an anti-climax! The psychological effect of going to one's death sitting on one's own coffin can only be imagined, but there is little doubt that the 20,000 strong crowd enjoyed the spectacle. A trip to a Town Moor execution would end in a picnic and frequently a drinking spree. From time to time condemned prisoners provided a little entertainment for the mob, and there was often good natured competition among them to determine who could impress the crowd the most. Some sang, others protested their innocence in verse form, while Henry Jennings – hanged for horse stealing in August 1786:

> gave an explanation of the cant terms used by robbers and pickpockets etc which he desired to be published for the benefit of the public

It was a public-spirited gesture and no doubt the good citizens of Newcastle appreciated it. Armed with the vocabulary of the criminal subculture, they could then more effectively tackle the problem of the highwaymen who were sorely plaguing the outskirts of the town.

Dozens of highwaymen ended their days dangling from a Town Moor gibbet. The last moments of one of them have been recorded in a broadsheet.

Jim O'Neil's Last Dance – 1816

> The cart stopped, and on being drawn under the gallows, O'Neil addressed a few words to his two brothers. He gave one a handkerchief and a watch. He then embraced and took affectionate leave of them. He shook hands with the jailors and executioner.

The cap was drawn over his head and after a few private ejaculations he was suspended. The executioner fulfilled his office well. O'Neil's struggles were short and there was but one convulsion of nature

The Barber Surgeon in attendance proclaimed O'Neil to be dead. His corpse was handed over to his family and friends who promptly carted it off to a nearby pub to be 'waked'. The boisterous wake continued until the early hours of the morning. When it was over, the corpse was carried back to St Andrew's Churchyard for burial.

O'Neil's treatment after death was exceptional in that the bodies of most condemned criminals were handed over to the Barber Surgeons for dissection. Another exception was William Winter hanged for the murder of an old lady in 1791. His crime was considered to be so heinous that his body was taken up to Steng Cross (near Elsdon and almost within sight of the murder) and then gibbeted. The body was placed within a metal cage and simply left to rot. When the corpse finally disintegrated, the bones were buried at its foot. Winter still has an odd grave marker, for a twenty-five foot high replica (complete with head) now marks his resting place.

PRISONS AND EXECUTION SITES

The fact that for most of its history Newcastle has had two prisons is explained by the granting of county status for the town in the year 1400. Prior to this date, Newcastle had merely been a large Northumbrian town under the legal jurisdiction of the Sherrif of the County. The granting of separate county status enabled Newcastle to hold its own courts in the Guildhall, and to maintain its own prison in the Newgate Barbican. Meanwhile the Castle Bailey and the buildings therein continued as an island of Northumbrian jurisdiction and the focus for law and order in that county. This duality extended to places of execution too. Northumbrian prisoners were executed at Westgate while Newcastle's miscreants were hanged on the Town Moor. The last public execution there took place in 1844 when Mark Sherwood was hanged for murdering his wife (public executions were nationally outlawed in 1868). After that date, all executions were carried out within the confines of the New Gaol in the Carliol district of Town. Newcastle and Northumberland continued to hold separate courts until an amalgamation took place in 1885.

The Castle as a Prison 1400-1812

Northumbrian malefactors were tried by the

Sherrif in the Castle Hall (the site now covered by the former County Hall). Following sentence they would be hauled off to the vaulted ground floor of the Keep known as the 'Guardroom'. Here it is still possible to see the shackles that were used to bind them, and it is not difficult to imagine the dreadful conditions in which they existed. These conditions appalled reformer John Howard when he visited the Castle in 1777, and he was highly critical of the authorities. Not only was the prison dark, cold and filthy but on certain days the place was thrown open to the public when for a 6*d* admission charge, selected prisoners were put on show like animals at a zoo. It was bad enough that decent debtors had to exist side by side with vicious criminals, but what really horrified Howard was the way in which the sexes were freely allowed to mix within the walls. This, Howard noted, should not be allowed to happen in a Christian country. Had he learned that in 1625 a child had been 'begotten in the Castell jail', I wonder?

The escape of 'Jock Armstrong of the Side' from the Castle on the eve of his execution, has been the subject of a celebrated border ballad. Jock had been instrumental in securing the escape of a number of Elizabethan Lords implicated in the 1569 Rebellion against the Queen known as the Rising of the North. Jock was treacherously betrayed and he fell into the hands of the Castle garrison who swore to hang him the next day. During the hours of darkness, the Armstrongs of Liddesdale mounted a daring guerilla raid in the course of which Jock was rescued and spirited off to the borders with the Castle garrison in hot pursuit.

Unfortunately there is little factual evidence to support this dramatic story. The leading characters do seem to have existed and the Castle was certainly in disrepair in 1569 but it is just possible that confusion has arisen between an escape attempt in that year and a curious episode in 1527 – an event that can be verified from several sources.

In 1527 the Scottish Regent Angus (husband of the widowed Margaret, wife of James IV) sought the arrest of Sir William Lisle for his part in a conspiracy. Lisle and his son Humphrey fled to Newcastle in an effort to escape the wrath of Angus. However, the Scottish Regent had influence south of the border and the Lisles, father and son, were clapped into the Castle to await an uncertain fate. They appear to have been held in one of the prisons adjoining the Black Gate and were fully determined to escape. They are known to have overcome their guards and to have gone on to free other prisoners. Rejoicing in their freedom, general mayhem ensued as they all embarked on an orgy of destruction:

They brake the prison wherein they were themselves put with divers other prisoners

Accounts relating to the damage caused as a result of this incident still exist. Eventually tiring of this occupation, William, Humphrey and their new-found allies made their way to the borders where they were readily welcomed by the Armstrongs.

For the next two years, William became an 'honorary' Armstrong, riding and reiving on a regular basis with them but in 1529 he rode one raid too many. Once again he fell into the hands of the Newcastle garrison. This time they took no chances. He was strung up immediately.

Westgate Gallows

In medieval times, the Skinnerburn ran just outside the West Gate of the town thus marking the boundary between Newcastle and Northumberland. The gibbet stood on its western side, the junction of Westgate and West Walls. Condemned prisoners were brought from the Castle, and a great many of them seem to have been captured reivers. William Winter was among those who died here in 1791 (see page

12). The West 'gait' was the main route into town from Carlisle and Hexham. Many a carter would have struggled in through the gate at dusk to glimpse his first friendly Novocastrian face – that of some unfortunate person swinging from the gibbet.

The Newgate Prison

Newgate was of necessity one of the strongest town gates in Europe. It straddled the road north and would therefore be the first to face the fury of attacking Scots armies. From 1400 onwards it served a dual role as both fortification and common jail of Newcastle. A vaulted room stood on each of its three storeys, while the walls were riddled with mural chambers, and it was within these rooms that the prisoners were housed. In sharp contrast to the Castle, Howard found Newgate to be warm, clean and well ventilated. There was also a small garden where inmates could take some fresh air. Even the condemned cell in the ground floor of the Barbican was pleasantly whitewashed.

Despite its air of impregnability, the Newgate was not a purpose-built prison and there were a large number of quite embarrassing escapes. Wily prisoners wormed their way down sewers or clambered out of the chimneys (in the year 1800 one stout prisoner became wedged tight and so he was recaptured). Tom Tate escaped the easy way.

Tom Tate had been employed as a Newgate Turnkey. His downfall began when he took to theft in order to supplement his meagre wages. Tom was apprehended and imprisoned in Newgate in June 1736.

Tom knew every nook and cranny of Newgate and he was fully cogniscent with both its strengths and its weaknesses. How he must have smiled to himself when he discovered that he was to be incarcerated in one of the cells adjoining the toll house on the Great North Road. One evening, Tom arranged for some of his cronies to be concealed inside the toll house – a small lean-to building. At the dead of night, these accomplices helped Tom and a felon named Ogle, to burrow through the ancient crumbling walls. Eventually they managed to hollow out an aperture wide enough to enable them to squeeze their way out to freedom. Once outside in the surrounding fields, the accomplices helped Tate and Ogle to remove their shackles. At this point most people would have made good their escape, but not Tom Tate. His prison clothing was bedraggled and likely to impede his chances of succesful escape, and most of his belongings still remained where he had left them on the day of his arrest – in the Jailer's House. Together

34

with Ogle, Tate broke in through a ground floor window.

Once inside, Tate made his way to his old lodgings and removed a chest containing his finest clothes. Ogle and Tate donned these clothes before clambering back out again unobserved. Sad to relate, he who dares does not always win. Tate was recaptured forty miles away near Bellingham, tried for theft and sentenced, but this time he was put in a prison from which escape was impossible – a prison ship bound for America.

The Town Moor Gallows

The Town Moor gallows tended to be a temporary structure, erected when demand required it. A variety of sites were used, but one of the favourite places stood north west of Fenham Barracks at the junction of Hunters and Barrack Roads. The gallows usually had a brief life span for a very different reason. The chewing of wood chips from a gibbet was a traditional cure for toothache and no doubt the Town Moor gallows disappeared by the mouthful after each execution.

Chapter Two

RESTLESS NATIVES

Newcastle can be lively at the weekend. The Bigg Market, bordered for centuries with hostelries, and now with wine bars, has always been a social focus. From time to time, then as now, matters appear to have got out of hand. A 1745 edition of the *Newcastle Courant* makes mention of:

> several outrages and disorders that have lately been committed in the Bigg Market

Twenty-eight culprits were rounded up. The four worst offenders were 'whipt', one was sent for a soldier (in what seems to have been an eighteenth century National Service Scheme) and four more were sent to the house of correction. The remainder were returned to their respective parishes for punishment.

Juvenile delinquency is not a twentieth century phenomenon. Unruly behaviour was endemic to the taverns and gambling dens of old Newcastle. As early as 1546 the Earl of Warwick noted the corruptive influence on his troops and he set up a gibbet at its head, to frighten them into mending their ways. Trouble, too, was always to be found in the 'red light' areas of the Quayside. Aeneas McKenzie, historian of Newcastle, writing in the 1820s, felt obliged to warn his readers of the 'Cyprian nymphs' who frequented this part of town, pointing out that these ladies were 'dangerous' but 'not very tempting'.

BRAWLS, DUELS AND RIOTS

In this rough environment, brawls were an everyday occurrence, some with serious consequences. In 1752, in Pinkney's Ale House in the Bigg Market, a local man began taunting Ewan MacDonald (a soldier in Guise's Regiment) with anti-Scottish jokes. A fight ensued and MacDonald stabbed his tormentor to death. Later that same year a ship's Surgeon – Henry Douglas – fought with one Edward Holliday. Ironically it was the Surgeon who was left slumped and bleeding to death in a Quayside chare. In both cases the guilty persons were hanged, but hanging does not seem to have acted as a deterrent. Street brawls continued to break out, fascinating bystanders. Legally, brawls were for the lower classes, the wealthy fought duels.

A white cross painted on a traffic island marks the position where once stood one of the eighteenth century market crosses of Newcastle. At this White Cross in Newgate Street, a celebrated duel was fought in 1701.

John Fenwick of Rock in Northumberland was a landowner of some importance who also had mining interests. Ferdinando Forster of Bamburgh was an MP and member of the lesser gentry. Each was an anethema to the other.

When both men were invited to the same grand jury lunch at the Black Horse in Newgate Street, fellow guests expected a lively meal. Nor were they disappointed. A skirmish broke out at the table but friends tactfully restrained the two. The following morning however, chancing to meet at the White Cross, hostilities were renewed and, urged on by the gathering crowd, verbal abuse soon led to sword play. A fine display followed, neither gaining the upper hand until unexpectedly, Forster slipped and fell. Fenwick seizing his opportunity, ran him through with his sword and then, fearful of the consequences, fled and hid in nearby Gallow-gate. Later captured and tried for murder, he was found guilty and condemned to hang. The town authorities were afraid that Fenwick's unruly miners might attempt a rescue bid and so they hanged him within the Town Walls, at the White Cross.

Both the Black Horse and the White Cross are long gone now, but a reminder of the famous duel can still be seen in the Chancel of Bamburgh Church. Ferdinando's Tomb stands there, complete with sword, gauntlets and thick iron breastplate. Possessing such impressive military accoutrements, it seems ironic that Forster should have been killed in a civilian contre-temps.

Riot!

Prior to 1763 most of the townspeople lived in the densely populated riverside suburbs of Pandon and Sandgate. People needed to live near their work, and this work was concentrated around the River Tyne. As industrialisation accelerated, so the population increased caus-ing overcrowding and resultant social tensions. These would build up, reach a climax and then erupt into spontaneous outbursts against authority. At such times the Town Guard tended to take a passive position, waiting for tempers to cool. In November 1688 during celebrations at the accession of William III, the crowd, made aggressive with drink, toppled the recently installed equestrian statue of the deposed King James II into the river. No mean feat as it was made of lead, When order had been restored, the authorities prudently fished it out, and melted it down to make new church bells.

That incident stemmed from over-fervent loyalty to the new reigning house, combined with over indulgence in alcohol. The one day rebellion of 26th June 1740 was very different, and it forcibly demonstrated to the authorities, the power and capacity of an angry Newcastle mob.

A Rebellion of the Belly

There had been a poor harvest in 1740, and the situation was further aggravated by grain merchants restricting supplies in order to drive the prices even higher. In less than six months the price of wheat and rye – the staple foodstuffs of the poor – had risen 160%. While Mayor Fenwick and his fellow Aldermen – themselves corn merchants – rejoiced in this golden opportunity to maximise profits, the poor were starving. Discontent reached fever pitch. On the 9th of June, in desperation, a number of keelmen, aided by a band of Wearside pitmen, plundered a grain ship. The Corporation viewed this incident with alarm and dispatched Alderman Ridley to parley with the mob. To pacify them, Ridley agreed to price stabilisation – a vain promise as the merchants continued to restrict supplies.

Concluding that the town authorities were doing little to alleviate their distress, a deputation of keelmen and pitmen made their way to the Guildhall accompanied by a belligerent crowd. At Sandhill they found their way blocked by a hastily assembled body of militiamen. The atmosphere was electric, as the militiamen held back this vast chanting crowd. Suddenly a gun went off. A boy fell dead. The crowd was momentarily hushed; then a great roar arose as the mob stampeded through the militia and surged around the Guildhall. The Corporation, their confidence lost, retreated behind locked doors in a state of siege. Mayor Fenwick describes what happened next:

> Stones flew in among us from without thro' the windows like cannon shot...at length the mob broke in on us. They spared our lives indeed, but obliged us to quit the place, then fell to plundering.

There was some mindless violence, including

the destruction of valuable records, but the prime object of the riot was to obtain money for bread. The town 'hutch' or money box, with its several locks, was forced open and its entire contents of over £1,200 was distributed to the most needy. The poor in effect, giving to the poorer.

With the town in the rioters' hands, old scores could be settled. The militiamen were chased back to their barracks and the civic fathers were 'escorted' back to their homes. Prisoners were released from jail with much 'huzzaing and blowing of horns'. Shopkeepers were coerced into selling their merchandise at the price agreed by Alderman Ridley while the Wearside mining contingent:

> marched in great order through the Town with bagpipes playing, drums beating and dirty clothes fixed upon sticks by way of colours flying

Energies dissipated by nightfall, the crowd melted away. When belatedly, several troops of cavalry clattered into town from Morpeth and Alnwick, only a small number of rioters could be found. Forty were arrested, tried and transported for:

> feloniously taking money belonging to the
> Mayor and Burgesses

The fact that his money was the fruit of blatant
profiteering seems to have been overlooked.

Hell's Kitchen

Pubs there were a-plenty in Newcastle, some
with a bad reputation, some even worse but none
more notorious than the taproom of the Flying
Horse in the Groat Market. This room was
known as 'Hell's Kitchen' and was no place for a
fastidious clientele. The taproom was the regular haunt of a band of semi-mythological figures
known as the 'Newcastle eccentrics'. Their
names alone indicate the nature of this coterie.
There was: 'Cull Billy', Euphy Scott, 'Bold
Archy', 'Knack-kneed Mack', 'Owld Judy', Captain Starkey, 'Bugle-nosed Jack' and a temperamental mongrel known as 'Timour'. This
bizarre band of simpletons, tramps, and con-
men centred around the fiddler 'Blind Willie'
Purvis. Purvis, composer of 'Buy Broom
Besoms' was a talented musician, and the
keelmen of Sandgate appear to have cherished
him in recognition of his prowess.

Willie and his friends ensured that a Rabel-
aisian atmosphere prevailed in Hell's Kitchen.
Fights frequently broke out, but the landlord,

Ralph Nicholson, merely locked the doors on the fracas, reopening them when the fury had abated. He sensibly kept the four foot long poker chained to the wall. Despite their undoubted excesses, the regulars were democrats at heart, and every year they elected their own 'mayor' even going so far as to arrange a little banquet in his honour.

The pub itself was demolished at the turn of the century and Thomson House now occupies the site.

Cuckoo Jack

Among Blind Willie's friends was a character known as 'Cuckoo Jack'. His real name was John Wilson and he was an oarsman on the Mayor's barge. His sideline as a marine scavenger was far more lucrative however. After a lifetime spent on the river, Cuckoo Jack knew every shoal and shallow. Consequently he was able to predict where objects lost overboard might be found. For a fee, Jack would retrieve them and return them to their former owners.

As river traffic increased, so the demand for Jack's scavenging services became greater. The Tyne was a dangerous river and many lives were lost each year. The Corporation would pay Jack a sum of money for every body he managed to recover, but a larger fee was paid for corpses recovered in the more difficult waters below bridge than for those secured from above. Offered these terms, Jack was not the man to allow moral scruples to interfere with his financial betterment and it was almost certain that anyone falling in the river at the Quayside would be dead by the time he was fished out downstream.

One day as Jack was cleaning a grappling iron on the Quayside, a friend came running towards him shouting for help.

'How Jackie, quick! There's some gadgie [fellow] fallen in the river!'

Jackie merely looked up at him and said;

'Whey man, hadaway. Ah get more for a deed 'un. Let the bugger droon!'

ON THE WATERFRONT

Without a doubt the most colourful group of characters ever to grace the streets of Newcastle were the keelmen. They were a feature of riverside life for centuries as they ferried cargoes of coal from collieries to the collier vessels waiting in the Tyne. They were tremendously skilled seamen, and theirs was a trade in which good judgement was as valuable as brute strength. Working with the tide, they manned the keels, each holding about 20 tons of coal, all of which was loaded and off-loaded by hand. The keel itself was a long, oval shaped boat, powered by sail and operated by a skipper, two mates and a boy called a 'pee-dee'.

They were a close-knit group and their dress as well as their life-style set them apart from other townsfolk. Clad in bright yellow waistcoat, blue jacket and straw boater, they were easily recognised. The harsh life they led left neither the time nor the inclination for them to develop refinements. They were tough, uncouth with a well-developed flow of invective and their behaviour frequently seemed calculated to offend burgher sensitivities. At a time when atheism was severely punished, the keelmen were openly irreligious. When John Wesley implored them to repent, they turned on him and he narrowly escaped being hurled into the river. His protector was Mrs Bailes the fishwife. She put one brawny arm around him and wielding her fish-knife in the other, called out to the menacing crowd:

'If ony yen o' lift up another hand to touch ma canny man, ayl floor ye directly'

Sceptical about religion, the keelmen had scant

respect for authority either. Nine years after rifling the 'town hutch', feelings were running high on quite a different matter. The keelmen concluded that Tyneside ought no longer to be part of a Kingdom ruled by an imported German Monarch. Marching to Elswick, they declared that Charles Edward Stuart was 'the true and recognised King in Newcastle'. Considering that this mischievous act of defiance took place just four years after the bloody suppression of the '45 Jacobite Rebellion, the in-built (and in this case void) anti-authoritarianism of the keelmen becomes apparent. The Corporation is said to have offered a large reward for information regarding the identity of the ringleaders. To the desperately poor, this must have proved a strong temptation but the tight-knit community of Sandgate remained silent.

In times of peace, the keelmen enjoyed the protection of the all-powerful coal barons but during the Napoleonic Wars a new and terrible scourge entered their lives

How to Catch a Keelman

They've prest my dear Johnny,
Se sprightly and se Bonny,
Alas I shall never more dae weel O.

The kidnapping squad
laid hold o' my lad,
As he was unloading the keel O.
The Sandgate Lassie's Lament

Keelmen were skilled seamen and ferociously brave fighters – first rate material for the Royal Navy. Few volunteered however, and in 1793 the Admiralty began dispatching press gangs to Newcastle in order to persuade a few more recruits to join the Navy – willingly or not. The press gangs set up their headquarters in the Plough Inn, Spicer Chare (on a site now covered by the Law Courts). Here they were perfectly placed to sally forth and 'lift' any keelman who looked as if he had the makings of a good sailor.

As previously mentioned, the keelmen had a dissolute reputation, reinforced by their collective weakness for drink. Few realised that when drunk, they were at their most vulnerable. The officers in charge of the press gangs knew it, and they hired a network of informers to report on the whereabouts of potential 'recruits'. Usually they were solitary men who had foolishly lingered in their local tavern for one last drink. A press man would arrive in disguise and offer to buy his intended victim a jug of ale. The keelman would (naturally) accept. Whilst his attention was engaged elsewhere, a shilling would be dropped into his tankard unobserved. Meanwhile, the remainder of the press gang would gather nearby in a pre-arranged spot (the corner of Broad Chare was a favourite place) and at a given signal would rush into the tavern and carry off their victim. The reluctant recruit would be bundled on board a tender in the river and then taken to a ship bound for Portsmouth or the Nore. The recruit would be given no opportunity to contact his family and many a keelman disappeared never to be seen again. Great hardship could be caused by the 'lifting' of a breadwinner and in 1796 the poor rate rose to six shillings in the pound because of the great demand put upon it by the families of recruited keelmen.

Occasionally the press men did make mistakes. The story is told of how on one nocturnal swoop, a pressed man was discovered to be an American and was, therefore ineligible to serve in the Royal Navy. He was put ashore at North Shields to the dismay of the press gang. Another impressed keelman, witnessing this, approached the captain of the tender and said:

'Let me off an' all, canny lad, ahm a Yankee tae!'

However it would be quite erroneous to suggest that the press gangs were always successful. On the contrary, the coal barons hindered their progress and prevented the Corporation from giving more than minimal assistance to the naval officers. As for the keelmen, they introduced their own counter-measures which included drinking only from glass-bottomed tankards to avoid inadvertently taking the King's shilling. Had John Wesley's oft-repeated exhortations to sobriety been heeded, many a tragic lifting would have been avoided. On one occasion an impressed keelman outwitted his captors and ran down Broad Chare towards the river in an effort to escape. Once on the Quayside, he found his pursuers closing in all around him, and the river seemed to offer the only hope of escape. The keelman plunged into the Tyne and made good progress in swimming across. The Tyne is a treacherous river and as he began to tire, the current swept him away to his death.

However, the keelmen were fighting on their own territory and thus had a certain advantage over their adversaries. If the press gangs could be lured into the warren-like maze of Sandgate, the hunters would soon become the hunted. At a pre-arranged signal, men, women and children would spring out of concealment and pelt the press men with all manner of missiles. If caught, the press men would be given a severe beating before being subjected to public ridicule and humiliation. The men were marched through Sandgate with their jackets turned inside out and their officers obliged to 'ride the steng' – a tiny seat attached to the end of a long pole on to which the unfortunate officer would be strapped and:

> carried through the streets, exposed to the insults and assaults of an enraged populace, the women in particular bedaubing them plentifully with dirt etc.
>
> *Newcastle Journal* 23rd April 1760

It was not unusual for entire ship's companies to return home to deal with those who had informed upon them to the press gangs, and at least one crew was denied shore leave for fear of the revenge they might exact.

The end of the Napoleonic Wars in 1815, saw the threat of redundancy replace the threat of impress, as their employers and one-time allies the coal barons sought to introduce new technology to the coal trade. The great boom in demand for coal caused by industrialisation was accompanied by ever-increasing efforts to introduce mechanical staiths along the Tyne, enabling sea-going colliers to load direct instead of by keel. The keelmen were thus slowly squeezed out of a market which they had dominated for centuries. Fears for their livelihood and even survival caused them, in 1822, to make what amounted to a last stand.

Throwing Stones at Tom and Jerry

The great strike known as the 'long stop' began in October. There had been many other strikes involving keelmen, but this one was unprecedented on account of the bitterness with which it was conducted. Both sides in the dispute marshalled their allies, and the keelmen's cause gained a major boost when they enlisted the support of the seamen who normally manned the collier ships. On the other side, the army and the Royal Navy rushed to the support of the coal barons, and even mining engineers pledged their services. As the industrial dispute escalated, the warship *Swan* was moored in the Tyne with its guns pointing provocatively towards Sandgate.

Once the keelmen had secured the co-operation of the seamen, the coal trade ground to a halt. Prices rocketed and the London coal agents tentatively began to eye the Scottish markets as a replacement for coal from the Tyne. The seamen and keelmen blockaded the Tyne and the coal owners were faced with the problem of how to get the coal out of the river.

New technology provided a solution. Given that a steam engine could pull a line of chaldron waggons, could one not be mounted upon a boat and modified in order to pull keels? The decision made, Thomas Hedley's engine named 'The Thomas and Jeremiah' was fitted to a keel, its wheels being replaced with paddles. Thus the little engine was turned into a steam tug boat, ready to pull keels crewed by the military.

The *Tom and Jerry* first attempted to run the blockade on 2nd November 1822. The sight of this little craft chugging downriver pulling keels, naturally incensed the strikers. They responded by lining the river banks and pelting the engine with stones and filth. The *Tom and Jerry*, unused to its present task was temperamental and breakdowns were frequent. The keelmen would then gleefully wade out into the river and overturn the keels, tipping both coal and military guards into the water.

The *Tom and Jerry* was one of the few craft to run the blockade, and even then, less than 50 chaldrons of coal per day were leaving the river (a chaldron being approx. 20 tons), a negligible amount in comparison to the norm for 1822 of 2,200 tons per day. Even so, the fact that coal was being moved on the Tyne was sufficient to calm the nerves of the London agents. Faced with starvation, the keelmen were forced to negotiate to return to work on reduced terms. They went back in the first week of December without having achieved any of their aims.

In the wake of this defeat, the installation of staiths proceeded relentlessly and with no further interruption, causing the number of employed keelmen to fall dramatically throughout the nineteenth century. Only the above-bridge collieries provided some employment for them, but the building of Armstrong's Swing Bridge of 1876, robbed them of even this last foothold. Their day was over and their livelihood gone. This tough and irreverent group which had given so much colour and vitality to life on Newcastle's Quayside, passed into the history books. Sadly, no keel remains as a reminder of this memorable body, nor would they recognise Sandgate today. Their spirit however, lives on in the empire of song which they built up on the riverside:

Weel may the keel row that my laddie's in...

A PARCEL OF MURDERS

Newcastle's natives were often restless, but they rarely resorted to real violence. There are comparatively few records of murder in the town's long history, but those committed have retained their sense of intrigue, as the following selection illustrates.

Pop Goes the Keelman – the shooting of Robert Lindsay, 8th July 1764

Eighteenth century Sandgate had a lively reputation and life was never dull. Most of its houses were crowded into a narrow, riverside strip, with the result that there was little space and everyone knew everyone else's business. From time to time tensions would mount and even childish pranks could lead to tragic consequences as tempers flared.

At four o'clock one July morning in 1764, Mrs Stewart, a pawnbroker's wife was woken early by an unwelcome noise. On opening her bedroom window, she saw to her horror, a face leering back at her. Robert Lindsay, a well-known Sandgate delinquent, was perched on the back wall singing at the top of his voice.

Understandably, Mrs Stewart was not amused. She sternly commanded the young keelman to remove himself at once. Lindsay responded with a barrage of insults and continued with his song. Mrs Stewart lunged at him furiously with a pair of hearth tongs and Lindsay answered by smashing the window with his fist. At this point Mr Stewart joined the fray, and he brought his old blunderbuss with him.

Stewart called out to Lindsay that if he would not come down of his own accord, he would be forced to shoot him down. Lindsay was unmoved, and stayed put as Mrs Stewart somewhat inexpertly assisted her husband to load and prime the gun. Stewart fired a warning shot, or rather attempted to, but the powder merely fizzled in the pan. Once again the Stewarts loaded the gun and levelled it at Lindsay (who was by now prostrate with laughter) Stewart pulled the trigger and this time Lindsay laughed no more. Shot at close range, he fell quite dead.

The coroner brought in a verdict of wilful murder. Stewart was tried, found guilty and sentenced to death. The unfortunate pawnbroker was hanged on the Town Moor on the 27th of August and his body was handed over to the Barber Surgeons for dissection.

Poor Stewart paid a dear price for using unreasonable force in an unpremeditated incident. Others have found the wheels of justice to be infinitely more lenient however.

The Blood-Spattered Bank – The Savings Bank Murder 7th December 1838

The grandiose designs of Richard Grainger were destined to transform the centre of Newcastle and provide the first planned city centre in the country. The 1832 Royal Arcade was one of the earliest developments, and in siting it at the foot of Pilgrim Street, Grainger was gambling that the proposed railway station would be built nearby. Some of the most prestigious institutions in Newcastle sought premises there, and empty units were quickly filled. The Savings Bank was among the first to move in. Few present at its opening could have guessed that it would be the scene of a sensational murder that would be the source of controversy for decades. In the early hours of the 7th December 1838 smoke was spotted issuing from the inner room of the bank. The fire brigade was alerted and they forced their way into the building.

Once inside, peering through the smoke-laden darkness, the firemen spotted two prostrate figures. A candle was brought, and the sight it revealed chilled even the most hardened of men. Walls, carpets and furniture were spattered with blood, hair and brains. Whilst one of the two figures was apparently reviving, the other lay quite still. The dead man was Joseph Millie, a mild mannered clerk. His head had quite literally been shattered and the instrument of his death – a badly bent poker – lay nearby. The pockets of the corpse were found to have been filled with paper and clearly the fire had represented an attempt to dispose of the evidence of a murder.

Attention now centred upon the survivor, Archibald Bolam a 41-year-old actuary and highly respected bank official. Bolam claimed that he had been receiving a series of threatening letters, the last of which had been slipped under the bank door on the day of the murder. Fearful for the safety of his housekeeper, Mary Walker, Bolam had left the bank at the earliest opportunity to warn her to be on her guard. On his return to the bank that evening, he had found Joseph Millie lying on the floor of the deserted premises. Bolam insisted that at this point he had been attacked from behind by a man with a blackened face, and a desperate life or death struggle had ensued. Bolam claimed that his assailant had attempted to slit his throat, but at that moment Bolam had passed out, only to regain consciousness when the fire brigade forced their way in. Of the alleged assailant, no trace could be found.

Bolam's account was riddled with inconsistencies and contradictions. The firemen had been convinced that the actuary was only shamming unconsciousness, and made their suspicions clear from the start. Damage to Bolam's clothing did not correspond to the wounds on his body, nor could it be said that the wounds to his throat were consistent with a determined attempt to cut his throat. Witnesses testified that Bolam had indeed been the last man to see Joseph Millie alive. In short, there was enough circumstantial evidence to obtain a warrant for Bolam's arrest on a charge of murder.

Furthermore, between Bolam's arrest and his trial in August, a series of revelations emerged to suggest that Bolam was not the pillar of respectability he purported to be. His housekeeper was actually his mistress, he had gambling debts, and he frequented vice dens. It is not surprising that when his trial took place, the Guildhall was crammed to capacity.

Predictably enough, the counsel for the prosecution had little difficulty in unpicking Bolam's account, while the testimony of his housekeeper regarding the timing of his movements was exposed as a tissue of lies. Even so, the prosecution was unable to produce any satisfactory motive for Bolam to murder Millie, and the two men were known to have been on amicable terms on the day of the crime. Nor would the bank admit to any irregularities in the accounts which Joseph Millie might have uncovered with fatal consequences. The evidence against Bolam was entirely circumstantial – but in most people's opinion it was strong enough to ensure that Bolam would be found guilty and few would have given much for his chances of escaping the hangman. They reckoned without Judge Maule.

Judge Maule gave a final summing-up so favourable to Bolam that it can be seen to have persuaded the jury of his innocence. In the Judge's opinion there was no question of wilful murder. Either Bolam had committed manslaughter in a fit of frenzy for motive unknown, or else Bolam's version of events was truthful and the murder had been carried out by an unidentified assailant. The obedient jury brought in a verdict of manslaughter and Bolam was sentenced to transportation for life to Australia. In return, Bolam became famous and the *Journal* serialised his life story.

There is a remarkable postscript to this story. Should the reader visit the Botanical Gardens in Sydney, it is still possible to see a sundial presented by one Archibald Bolam 'one time citizen of Newcastle upon Tyne'. Little is known of this mid-nineteenth century benefactor, except that he was a self-made man. At his death he was buried in St Stephen's Church, Sydney. On his grave is an epitaph ending with the words:

Here lies an Honest Man

We shall never know the truth about Bolam, but we do know that the Royal Arcade, the scene of his crime, went into a gradual decline. The anticipated railway station was actually built at the foot of Grainger Street, and one by one the institutions pulled out (the Savings Bank moved to Grainger Street in 1862). In the mid-1970s a large scale replanning scheme called for the dismantling of the Royal Arcade, and the building of Swan House to replace it.

One last reminder of the past glories of the Royal Arcade does remain however, in the form of a smaller-scale replica incorporated in the ground floor of Swan House, The colourful stucco and expansive windows conjure up the elegance of a vanished age, yet the Arcade replica has a forlorn and somewhat disturbing atmosphere. There is no trace of the Savings Bank now. The site it occupied on the original Arcade is now taken up by the exit to the Tyne Bridge underpass in the replica.

The Blackett Street Murder
1st October 1861

Mark Frater, 51, was a man going places. One autumn morning as he briskly stepped off his bus and made his way to his Blackett Street office, the omnibus proprietor could not have guessed that he was about to make the longest journey of all.

Frater was a self-made man. After working for years as a tax collector, he finally amassed enough money to purchase the lucrative little bus service that ran between Bulman's Village (Gosforth) and the foot of Northumberland Street. The venture proved to be remarkably successful and Frater maintained an office at 2, Blackett Street (near the junction with Pilgrim Street). One fateful morning in 1861 as he stepped from his bus and walked the few paces to his office, Frater was unaware that he was being stalked by a maniac.

Blackett Street was as crowded in 1861 as it is today. As Frater picked his way through the knots of people, he spotted a friend and paused on the threshold of his office to speak a few words. Neither man caught sight of the surreal knife-wielding figure who suddenly seemed to loom up out of nowhere. The friend called out a warning. Frater spun around, but as he did so, the psychopath plunged the five-inch blade deep into his neck. Horrified onlookers pinioned the crazed attacker to the ground. Meanwhile Frater was carried to his office, blood gushing freely from his wound. Frater muttered, 'I'm afraid I'm done for'. He was right. He was placed in an armchair where he quietly and helplessly bled to death.

The murderer was George Clark, a cabinet maker who lived in a house overlooking St Nicholas Churchyard. It will be recalled that Frater had been a tax collector. It seems that he had been given the task of collecting an un-popular dog tax, and Clark who owned what was described in court as a 'mean-looking spaniel', refused to pay it. Frater was forced to distrain for the amount by confiscating Clark's cabinet-making equipment (an exercise fraught with danger as Clark already had a reputation for violence). In Clark's deranged mind, a grudge rapidly turned into murderous hatred. He began to follow Frater in order to build up a pattern of his movements. A suitable oppor-tunity arose on October 1st and Clark struck.

He was found guilty of wilful murder but it was apparent that Clark was criminally insane. The death sentence was commuted and thereafter he spent his remaining days in a lunatic asylum. Poor Frater not only lost his life to a madman, but the business he was so proud of was sold and went into decline. His office was demolished towards the end of last century and the block dating from 1895 was erected in its place.

'Wor Jin' – Murder in the Keelman's Hospital Jan 2nd 1829

Jane Jameson (better known as 'Jin') was a young woman who sold rags, fruit – and occasionally, her favours – at the Sandgate 'pant' or fountain. Alluring she was not, and a contemporary account describes her as:

A disgusting and abandoned female of most masculine appearance, generally in a state of half nudity.

Nor was Jin exactly what you might describe as an ideal neighbour. Not only was she usually blind drunk, but she was subject to fits of violent temper. Folk pointed out that her two illegitimate children had died in suspicious circumstances, while her loose-living made her the talk of Sandgate – and Sandgate folk were well used with excessive behaviour. There was some hope that Jin's attitude might improve when she went to live with her widowed mother in the Keelman's Hospital. The optimism proved to be misplaced.

Inmates of the Keelman's Hospital lived in comparative luxury compared to other nineteenth century townsfolk. Widows and dependants occupied neat self-contained apartments such as the one Mrs Jameson lived in, number Five on the ground floor of the Hospital. Despite the relative spaciousness of these apartments, it cannot easily be explained how the stoic Mrs Jameson was able to tolerate her wayward daughter's excesses within this confined space. In 1828 Jane actually moved her lover, Billy Ellison, into the room she shared with her mother. On New Year's Day 1829 tempers boiled over and matters came to a head with horrific consequences.

Jin and Billy had ventured forth on a Sandgate pub-crawl, when their money ran out. They returned to the Hospital in an effort to persuade Mrs Jameson to fund their continuing spree. Mrs Jameson refused. A quarrel broke out and soon the neighbours had their ears to the wall. The argument reached a climax when Mrs Jameson accused her daughter of having murdered her two children. Maddened with drink, Jin seized the red-hot poker from the fire, now slender and pointed through years of wear, and thrust it through her mother's heart.

Poor Mrs Jameson lingered for a few more days. Even in extremis she pathetically tried to shield Jin by claiming that the incident had been the result of an accident. She claimed to have tripped and fallen on the poker, thereby causing the injury herself. When she mercifully died, Jin, belatedly consumed with remorse, was arrested on a charge of murder.

At her trial in March, Jin could not afford a defence counsel and the judge had to cross examine prosecution witnesses himself. Somewhat unsportingly, Jane attempted to pin the blame upon Billy by claiming that he had viciously kicked her mother with one of his steel-capped shoes. A plethora of witnesses testified otherwise and Jin's fate was sealed. The judge urged the jury to show clemency, but Jin was found guilty of wilful murder and sentenced to be hanged. On March 7th, thirty year old Jin was taken to the Town Moor on a tumbril. The 20,000 strong crowd included many of her Sandgate cronies. Justice done, Jane was pronounced dead and her body cut down from the gallows. Oddly enough this was not the end of her story.

As previously mentioned, the bodies of condemned criminals were handed over to the Barber Surgeons for dissection, and Jin was duly carted off down to the Surgeon's Hall in the Manors District. On arrival, her corpse was displayed in the courtyard for several hours in front of a large crowd. Then the serious business began. Jane was plunged into a vat of boiling water, flayed and then displayed in such a way as to enable the celebrated Surgeon, John Fife to use her to illustrate anatomical lectures. The students enthusiastically picked over her corpse for several days, until finally they cremated what was left in the incinerator, the great chimney of which can still be seen near the premises at the head of Croft Stairs.

It was generally recorded that Jane Jameson faced trial and execution with more dignity than she had ever shown during her lifetime. Troublesome in life, composed at her execution, Jane, in death made a small but very real contribution towards furthering the cause of medical science, and one way or another, medical science was much in the news during the first quarter of the nineteenth century.

BARBER SURGEONS
AND BODY SNATCHERS

The Surgeon's Hall has long since disappeared, but we know of its appearance from contemporary prints. It was a fine classical building which dominated the surrounding slums of Pandon and Manors. When the medical students grew weary of dissecting cadavers, they could gaze out over the surrounding garden with its statues of the four great doctors of antiquity. Yet the ordinary folk of Newcastle remained immune to its charms, they knew of it only as a place of fear and menace – a place to be avoided. And no wonder! Read on!

Half-hanged Macdonald

Ewan Macdonald was a Highland soldier sentenced to death for murder in the eighteenth century. Upon mounting the gallows, the poor man's nerve gave way. As the noose was placed around his neck, he lashed out with his feet and knocked the hangman off the scaffold. The executioner dusted himself down and climbed back up. The second attempt to launch Ewan into eternity proved to be more succesful – or so the hangman thought.

Ewan's corpse was taken to the Surgeon's Hall, where a solitary medical student remained on duty. The student occupied himself with some task, suddenly he was alerted by groans where no groans should be...He turned, and to his amazement the 'corpse' was reviving. (Ewan may well have used the old trick of swallowing a tiny silver pipe prior to the noose being put in place). Soon the resurrected man was pleading for his life.

The student faced a real dilemma and he pondered the situation carefully. On the one hand he had no right to take life, but to release Ewan would mean losing a precious body. Besides which, Ewan was a condemned man, he would only be recaptured, rehung and dissected in another part of the country, thus being lost to Newcastle. It was too awful to contemplate! The student made up his mind and responded to Ewan's pleas by smartly bringing his mallet down on Ewan's head, thereby dealing him a fatal blow. The issue was decided. No self-respecting medical man could afford to have a corpse simply get up and walk away from him like that!

The student knew no remorse, rather he boasted of the incident to his colleagues. He could not have known that nemesis was at hand, albeit in a most unexpected form. Shortly afterwards, the apprentice unwisely approached a frisky horse which struck out at him with its hooves and killed the boy stone dead. The superstitious locals solemnly concluded that the beast had been possessed by Ewan's vengeful ghost. A more credible explanation might be that Ewan's colleagues in the army caught up with the apprentice and carefully but effectively bludgeoned him to death. So the legend of half-hanged Macdonald was born, and even as early as the eighteenth century, the Barber Surgeons had earned themselves an unenviable reputation.

It is not therefore surprising that few willingly lingered in the vicinity of the Barber Surgeon's Hall, and if by the middle of the nineteenth century the medical men felt aggrieved at this negative image, it was after all self-inflicted. Prior to 1832 medical science may have been in its infancy but it was making great strides, this despite the fact that corpses necessary for anatomical instruction were in short supply. Few men were as public-spirited as Cutler, the deformed pie-man.

John Cutler sold pies to the medical fraternity, and this brought him into contact with the celebrated Surgeon John Fife. Fife was fascinated with Cutler's mis-shapen body and he offered the princely sum of £10 in return for rights of dissection after death. Cutler was happy to oblige and considered this arrangement to be a good business deal. After all, he had made a living out of the medical men and now he had an opportunity to give something back to the profession.

Bodies always being in short supply, it was possible to earn up to ten guineas by bringing the Surgeons a 'good subject'. However few people followed the example of the mourners at a funeral described in the *Newcastle Courant* of 28th January 1826.

It seems that the deceased was of a miserly disposition and a small gathering of apathetic relatives and acquaintances gathered at his home prior to the funeral. Few among this unenthusiastic little group relished the prospect of having to sit through a long funeral service at St Johns, and along the route one by one they drifted away from the cortege, making their way to the Bigg Market taverns instead. Eventually only the coffin bearers were left following the vicar. Realising the situation, and determined to make the best of a bad job, they promptly turned around and, still bearing the coffin, made their way down to the Surgeon's Hall where they sold both coffin and contents for beer money!

With the demand for fresh corpses continually outstripping supply, it is not surprising that

there was a booming corpse trade. This trade –
often encouraged by the no-questions-asked
attitude of distinguished medical men in receipt
of its supplies – brought terror and despair to
communities in the North of England and the
Scottish Lowlands. Parishioners responded to
this threat by erecting railings such as those still
to be seen surrounding All Saints Churchyard.
How frustrating it must have been for the
medical men in the Barber Surgeon's Hall to

witness funeral services take place at nearby All Saints, and how tempting to plan a nocturnal foray aimed at unearthing some newly-interred corpse to work on...In fact the proximity of the overhanging houses in All Saints Churchyard coupled with the railings, precluded any body snatching there. The dreaded 'resurrection men' much preferred to remove corpses from sparsely populated areas such as Elswick and the Ballast Hills. Heavy metal cages called 'mort-safes' were frequently placed over fresh graves and the people of Morpeth even erected a watch tower in their local churchyard.

Such precautions were fully justified, and events focusing on the Turf Inn were to conclusively demonstrate just how extensive this operation actually was.

Rent-a-Corpse Ltd.

The premises of Lloyd's Bank occupy a palazzo-like block on the south side of Collingwood Street. This block replaced the Turf Hotel which was, in its heyday one of the most important coaching inns in the North of England, for the Turf was the focal point for daily coaches bound for York and Edinburgh. In religious deference these services did not run on Sundays, and it was this factor which revealed Newcastle's role in the corpse-smuggling trade.

The Turf Hotel Booking Office served as a storing place for all manner of merchandise awaiting onward carriage, and at busy weekends it was common for packages to miss the designated coach. This happened one Saturday in September 1825, and the following day staff became alarmed by a foul smell emanating from a certain large box. The case in question was addressed to one 'James Syme, 6 Forth Street, Edinburgh'. Staff were suspicious enough to summon the police and the case was gingerly opened in the presence of a magistrate. The case was found to contain the body of a teenage girl. There were no signs of voilence and the coroner recorded a verdict of death by natural causes. The girl's identity was not established and she was buried in an unmarked pauper's grave in St John's Churchyard. This was destined to be only the first of a series of grim discoveries made by the staff of the Turf. In almost identical incidents, no less than four bodies were found in cases bound for the Edinburgh coach, and every time things appeared to be returning to normal, yet another corpse would turn up. Working in the Turf became a traumatic and deeply disturbing occupation. Meanwhile the police puzzled over the provenance of these itinerant corpses.

A body discovered on Christmas Day 1828 was traced back to the interment of a little girl in

Whitekirk near York. The child had been buried just on Christmas Eve and once again the destination was an Edinburgh one – in this case 'John Smith, 33 York Place, Edinburgh'. A second series of corpse discoveries had begun. On Thursday 8th of January 1829, a man described as a 'soft spoken Scotsman' deposited a large box in the Booking Office of the Queen's Head, Pilgrim Street (now restored as 'Alderman Fenwick's House'). Suspicious staff opened the case and found the pathetic corpse of a child, Lizzie Mills, a shoe-maker's daughter who had been buried in the Ballast Hills graveyard in Newcastle, just a couple of days previously. Policemen rushed to the grave, but there were only minimal signs of disturbance. Clearly the resurrection men were expert at their ghastly trade, and we will never know how many other Novocastrians were raised from their eternal sleep, wrapped as hellish parcels and then put on a coach bound for Edinburgh.

In November 1828 a man brought a suspicious looking parcel to the Turf. The box contained a body and the man was arrested. He gave his name as 'James Aitcheson' and stated that his native town was Edinburgh. Claiming that he had merely been paid to deliver the box and pleading ignorant as to its contents, gained the gentleman an acquittal. A day later a shopkeeper came forward with information that 'Mr Aitcheson' had actually bought wood from him to make the case. Obviously the mysterious Mr Aitcheson knew a great deal more of this affair than he had been prepared to admit. A second arrest warrant was issued, but predictably enough, he had disappeared without a trace, leaving only the red faces of police and magistrates in his wake.

Curiously, it was events north of the border that were destined to shed some light on this murky trade. The notorious duo Burke and Hare had taken body-stealing to its logical conclusion by murdering vagrants to ensure a constant supply of bodies for the Edinburgh anatomists. Their sensational trial in December 1828 revealed that Hare had actually been in Newcastle that same year. Had he been instrumental in creating a corpse supply network that centred upon Newcastle and operated throughout the Northern English Counties? One thing seems certain, the corpses that were discovered in Newcastle probably only represented the tip of a very unpleasant iceberg.

As for the staff of the Turf, understandably they became increasingly reluctant to open suspicious boxes. In November 1828 one such case arrived on a coach from York. Mindful of past experiences, the porters refused to unload the case in question, and it was still on board as the York coach made its return journey. Staff in York were equally unwilling to assume responsibility for the evil-smelling box and they promptly put it back on the next Newcastle-bound coach. We can well imagine the thoughts of the long-suffering Turf staff as the dreaded case reappeared on top of the York coach. Legend has it that a disgusted porter finally took the box and hurled it into the River Tyne.

By 1832 the day of the body stealer was over. The passing of the Anatomy Act rendered their services unnecessary. Faced with mushrooming industrial cities and a mid-century population explosion, central governments had passed a number of measures aimed at more efficient social regulation. Medical Science was not forgotten and the Anatomy Act was designed to ensure a steady supply of corpses for medical research. This may have seemed to be commendable enough on the surface, but the Act cut through one of the more humane conventions of parish responsibility. Traditionally, when a family was too poor to bury a relative, that relative could be registered as officially 'unclaimed'. In these circumstances the parish would sympathetically assume the cost of burial in a pauper's grave. With the passing of the Anatomy Act however, all corpses remaining unclaimed 48 hours following death could be possessed by the local medical school and dissected. In theory the Anatomy Act represented a logical remedy to solve the problems caused by the demand for fresh corpses, in practice it penalised the poor for simply being poor. And by mid-century there were a great many poor people living in Newcastle.

Newcastle was, by 1850 at its economic zenith as one of the most important ports in the world. The concentration of mining, shipping and engineering concerns held the promise of work for the poorer classes. Thousands of immigrants, many of them Irish, poured into the city in the hope of finding employment as casual workers. Being unskilled, they were given the very worst housing and most eked out an existence of sorts in the slums of Pandon and Sandgate. Omnipresent disease in these areas ensured a high death rate and thus a steady supply of corpses for research. The old Barber Surgeons had by now given way to the Newcastle Medical School. A thirst for knowledge among the students gave the Medical School the reputation of being a little over-zealous in its interpretation of the Anatomy Act. Whenever news reached them of some poorhouse inmate in extremis, the Medical School handcart would soon be waiting patiently outside.

Mrs Rox – A Lady in Demand

On 7th December 1840 Mrs Rox died in All Saints Workhouse. Her impoverished family naively sought a burial 'on the parish' and did not claim her body. The gamble failed and the Medical School porters were quickly (as it happens a little too quickly) on hand to whisk Mrs Rox off to the Surgeon's Hall for dissection.

The Rox family were devout Roman Catholics and as funerals and wakes were necessary and satisfying family rituals, we can well imagine their outrage on learning of the proposed fate of Mrs Rox. Soon Pandon was in a state of uproar. The mid-nineteenth century Newcastle civic fathers were not normally noted for taking the feelings of unfranchised slum-dwellers into consideration as they deliberated on weighty matters of office, but the Rox family were fortunate in that the Medical School, and in particular its renowned Surgeon John Fife, had made enemies in high places. Fife was a political radical with Chartist sympathies and he had twice served as Lord Mayor of Newcastle, but the present incumbent of that post was Fife's arch-rival John Carr. When Carr learned of the disturbing events in Pandon he seized the opportunity to make political capital against Fife who was, of course, closely associated with the Medical School. Carr gave his support to the Rox family cause and agreed to spearhead a march upon the Surgeon's Hall.

The volatile mob descended upon the Medical School with Carr at its head. As the terrified staff retreated behind locked doors, Carr strode forward calling out:

'You've got a body in here. Open these doors or I'll break them in.'

Nervously a surgeon replied:

'Er, yes but we obtained it legally, really we did! er, didn't we?'

Mayor Carr turned red with rage and bellowed out:

'It shan't be done here! I won't allow this in my town! Why, why, you'll be taking the living next!'

The doors of the school were reluctantly opened and in swarmed the excitable Pandon mob. They entered the dissecting room and found the corpse of Mrs Rox about to be plunged into a vat of boiling water. Seizing the body, they replaced it in its rough deal coffin and trundled it back up the hill to All Saints Church for immediate Mass and burial.

In February 1841 the magistrates found the Medical School porters guilty of taking possession of Mrs Rox's body before the statutory 48 hours had elapsed after death. Fines were levied on the staff as individuals but the Medical School was obliged to pay them, after all the porters had acted upon instructions from their superiors. The affair was over. Carr scored a significant propaganda victory over Fife, and the Rox family obtained a decent burial for their mother. Honour was satisfied on both sides.

As most of this chapter has centred upon the anti-authoritarianism of Novocastrians, it is perhaps fitting to end it on a rare note of harmony between Mayor and common people.

Chapter Three

PLAGUE AND DISASTER

PESTILENCE!

For most of the Town's long history, the inhabitants of Newcastle lived in narrow riverside districts hemmed in by both the Tyne and the constricting medieval wall. These conditions, allied to the fact that hygiene was not one of our ancestors' strong points, resulted in Newcastle suffering from the same problems that blighted Europe as a whole.

The town's water supply was drawn from the numerous open cisterns that could be found in the market places and at such focal points as the Newgate and Cale crosses. Erratic of supply and contaminated with germs, this water was shared with the local livestock as well. The Tyne was the most obvious source of drinking water, but as the centuries progressed, the river became increasingly murky and by the close of the nineteenth century, to drink water from the river was tantamount to committing suicide.

If the water supply left much to be desired, little thought had been allocated to street cleaning either. In time honoured tradition, rubbish was simply hurled out of windows and passers-by risked being showered in all manner of filth as they picked their way through the narrow chares. The Corporation only accepted responsibility for cleaning the principal thoroughfares, and they established a gargantuan midden in the redundant Castle ditch. This heap was so substantial that during the famous 1644 Siege, Mayor Marley ordered that it be carted away and used as backing for the hastily patched-up Town Wall. Sadly for the people of Newcastle, not even a mountain of dung could prevent the Scots from taking the town that October.

Meanwhile the Lort Burn and its little valley (now covered by Dean Street) offered a handy substitute for those who could not face the long climb up to the Castle Garth. The burn threaded its way through the centre of the walled town and its tangled, foetid depths emitted a nauseous stench.

In short, the Newcastle of old – however picturesque it may look in contemporary illustrations – was a breeding ground for all manner of deadly bacteria, and infectious (zymotic) diseases such as typhus, scarlet fever, diarrhoea, diptheria, measles and smallpox, all took their annual toll on the population. An additional factor made the situation even more acute. Newcastle was a seaport and deadly disease could just as easily be imported as home grown.

The Jolly Rant

Newcastle suffered with the rest of the country in the first visitation of bubonic plague of 1345-

1349 – later to be called the Black Death. Once the plague, introduced by black rats, had established itself in a locale, it would then spread rapidly, abate, and then return with even greater virulence than before. Symptoms varied with the strain involved, but the tell-tale signs were fever accompanied by black swellings of the glands about the groin and armpits. The accompanying delirium led to Northerners referring to this disease as 'the jolly rant'. There was little joviality once infected and few survived the onset of illness.

In town, the death toll amongst the master masons was so great that rebuilding work on the Nave and Transepts of St Nicholas' Church was halted for many years. Although the disease abated in the fifteenth century, the closing years of Elizabeth's reign saw its return with several major outbreaks throughout the seventeenth century. Bearing in mind that the population of Elizabethan and Stuart Newcastle stood around 10,000 people, the epidemics were indeed severe.

Recorded in 1579 – 2,000 deaths
Recorded in 1589 – 1,700 deaths
Recorded in 1636 – 5,037 deaths

Predictably enough, the poor and weak bore the

brunt of the onslaught The Parish Register of St John's Church contains the following entry for 1589:

Edward Errington – Town Fool – died in peste

and for 1591:

April 7th A poore woman dieing in the donghill – buried

Contagious disease knows no class distinctions and the entry for December of 1589 suggests that some important people fell victim to the plague too:

Died thes month Mr. Wm Selbie (mayor) and John Gibson (sherrif)

The 1636 outbreak emanated from the crew of a Dutch ship which had docked on the Tyne. Before the plague subsided several months later, half the population of Newcastle was dead.

Faced with this major epidemic, the town fathers appointed a 'plague man' – an official charged with identifying the sick and ensuring the removal of the dead and dying. In his distinctive garb of grey robe with peaked hood, the sight of this ghostly half-glimpsed figure gliding down the narrow chares in the dead of night, must have seemed like a vision of Death himself. The trail of empty houses he left in his wake was eloquent testimony of the tenants' fate. The 'plague man' was empowered to enter any house irrespective of the owner's status. An infected house would be identified with a cross painted on the door, and the interior would be cleansed with a mixture of burning pitch, frankincense and resin. The sick and the dying would be carted off to one of the nearby shanty towns which grew up overnight at Spital Tongues and St Annes. A number of burial pits have been discovered at these places over the years, and bones discovered in the course of some eighteenth century developments in Northumberland Street, may also be evidence of hastily buried plague victims.

Despite all official efforts, the sheer scale of the epidemic left the authorities helpless. Contemporary reports tell of people dying in the streets and of grass growing in the once bustling chares. There can be little doubt that organisation broke down and Newcastle must have taken years to recover. It has been suggested that the children's rhyme 'Ring a Ring a Roses' represents a popular enshrinement of both the symptoms and the effects of the plague. A 'pocket full of posies' probably alludes to a pomade of herbs and flowers – a traditional means of staving off plague, while the 'ring of roses' suggests the red skin rash which often accompanied the first symptoms of bubonic plague. The final line 'Atishoo, Atishoo, we all fall down' is a metaphor pointing to the inevitable fate of the plague victim, and it invests this seemingly innocent children's verse with a far grimmer significance.

The threat of bubonic plague finally ended when brown rats vanquished the disease-carrying black ones, but in the nineteenth century, Europe was threatened by a scourge just as deadly, and this at a time when Newcastle was well on its way to becoming one of the busiest seaports in the world.

A Court for King Cholera

Cholera is possibly the most terrible of all contagious diseases. It is caused by the victim drinking water contaminated by the cholera morbus. At first the victim suffers shivering and stomach cramps, followed by a phase of violent convulsions as the patient's circulatory system collapses. Within three to four days the victim is likely to be dead. Such is Asiatic cholera. In the 1830s King Cholera left his native shores and proceeded to cut a swathe through Europe. At this stage, Newcastle was one of only a handful of

British towns to have remained immune from cholera, but unknown to the authorities, a time bomb was steadily ticking away within their town, ironically enough, a time bomb placed by the authorities themselves.

Keeping Newcastle's mushrooming population supplied with drinking water had always been problematical. By 1832 this problem had been made more acute by droughts evaporating the water held in the town's reservoirs. In an attempt to counter a water shortage, the well-meaning civic fathers sanctioned the new Water Subscription Co. to pump water directly out of the Tyne at Elswick and sell it from handcarts. As, at this time nobody associated disease with contaminated water, the knowledge that the intended drinking water was actually being pumped from one of the most heavily polluted parts of the Tyne, caused no sleepless nights. What the Authorities did not realise was that those waters were already infected with the cholera morbus. King Cholera had come to town.

Oswald Reay, died in October 1831 and he was to be only the first of many. To avoid causing a panic, the authorities initially denied the presence of cholera, and by the time their emergency measures were put into operation, the disease had a firm grip upon Newcastle.

As 20-40 new cases were reported each day, business on the river ground to a halt because quarantine measures had to be introduced to safeguard river traffic. The existing hospitals – the Infirmary, Fever Hospital and Dispensary were soon crammed to capacity and emergency 'hospitals' were opened in the parish poor-houses. Social events were cancelled that autumn and an unlikely New Year's Eve curfew was introduced with reasonable success. Attitudes towards the epidemic varied. Fired with an Evangelical dread of a God of Wrath, many regarded the disease as divine vengeance upon a Godless and increasingly materialistic society. The more hedonistic took refuge in the alleged properties of alcohol as a means to keep cholera at bay. Old servicemen recommended eating rice, and many an anxious nanny stuffed her infant charge with copious quantities of tapioca as a result. The epidemic offered opportunities for the unscrupulous as well as for rice importers and contemporary local newspapers contain advertisements for such dubious concoctions as Dicey's Genuine 'Daffy's Elixir'.

Alternatively there was always 'Barnes Anti-Cholera Morbus Tincture' selling at the outrageous price of £1 10s 6½d per bottle (the average weekly wage was only 15s).

At first, the middle class readership tended to

take a somewhat relaxed view of the epidemic. The *Newcastle Chronicle* was of the opinion that the morbus was likely to infect only:

> the lowest class living in crowded tenement appartments and addicted to habits of intemperance

This complacency was to have fatal consequences for those of any class who came into contact with contaminated water. Among those who died as the disease worked its way through the well-heeled quarters of Eldon Square and Northumberland Street, was the much respected Newcastle historian and political radical Aeneas Mackenzie.

The people of Newcastle grew accustomed to the incessant tolling of the death bell and the smell of lime-washed chares. Special areas were put aside in each parish churchyard for the burial of victims and the very poor were buried in mass graves. In St Nicholas Churchyard, 31 people were buried near the North Transept (close to the present statue of Queen Victoria), while in All Saints, 87 people were interred in a wretched plot overlooking Silver Street Stairs. At last, in March the outbreak subsided and life gradually returned to normal. We will never know the real death toll as the authorities only acknowledged deaths that took place from December 1831. The official figure was 306 deaths, though we can be sure that the real figure was far higher.

Ten years later, Edwin Chadwick published his pioneering work emphasising the link between sanitation and disease. In Newcastle the authorities gave an apathetic response and continued to sanction the pumping of water from the Tyne for drinking purposes. By mid-century they had, after all, more pressing social problems to deal with. Since 1832 the population of the Town had rocketed from 55,000 to 90,000 and, as most of these migrants were housed in the already overcrowded suburbs of Sandgate and Pandon, the ensuing congestion presented an insoluble problem to a Corporation which had hitherto never concerned itself with the housing conditions of the lower classes. A series of local acts had been passed which now empowered the Corporation to regulate overcrowding, oversee planning and inspect properties but the authorities paid as much attention to these as they had to Chadwick's Report. In the Summer of 1853 the inevitable happened and cholera returned to ravage the grim tiers of riverside tenements. In many ways the episode was a carbon copy of the disaster of 1832, only this time the Corporation could not plead ignorance to the dangers of supplying contaminated water, and 1,533 people paid for it with their lives.

DISASTER!

In the course of the centuries, Newcastle has suffered a catalogue of disasters that read like the fate meted out to some latter day Sodom and Gomorrah. To the scourge of plague, we must also add flood and fire.

There is an old saying that a river is a good provider but a cruel master. Just as the Tyne was Newcastle's *raison d'être* so the river from time to time has almost proved to be the town's undoing. In the reign of Edward III (1327-77), the district of Pandon was one of the most important parts of the old town, largely on account of the concentration of princely merchants who chose to live there. Pandon was low-lying and prone to flooding from both the Tyne and the Pandon Burn which flowed through the area. The houses, of timber construction built upon a framework of stakes driven into the silt, would have been vulnerable to flood. This vulnerability was demonstrated on 15th August 1339 when the river burst its banks and flooded Pandon with catastrophic results. Chroniclers recorded that over 140 people lost their lives as the floodwater undermined the timber staiths.

Quite apart from the loss of life, the flood must have caused a great deal of damage to the economy of Newcastle and the decision to build a more permanent stone quay (first mentioned in 1376) was probably taken as a result. The site of the disaster is now covered by the Law Courts and the whole area has changed beyond medieval recognition. The Pandon Burn, however, is still there far beneath the buildings. Although now tamed by a conduit, the burn, following heavy rain, can still pose a problem to light craft attempting to moor on the river at Burn Bank Stairs.

A Disappearing Landmark – The Great Flood of 1771

The bridge over the Tyne was one of the few structures to have survived the Great Flood of 1339 – albeit in a damaged form. It was duly repaired and went on to serve the good people of Newcastle for many more centuries. The bridge was, of course, Newcastle's *raison d'être*. It had been the stage of events both stirring and pathetic and a myriad of historical personalities had passed over it at one time or another. Providing a link with Durham and the South, the bridge was a lucrative site to own a shop, and by 1771 had been colonised by a number of shopkeepers who proceeded to hollow out cellars from the bridge pillars and to cantilever their shops perilously out over the parapet. These alterations may have given the bridge a picturesque appearance, but protracted interference with the bridge supports seriously weakened the structure. The scene was set for disaster and in November 1771, following a period of prolonged rainfall, the level of the Tyne rose by six feet and the swollen waters swirled dangerously around the abutments.

At two o'clock in the morning, people living near the river were awoken by a terrible noise above the roar of the rushing waters could be heard the unmistakeable sound of straining timbers and sliding masonry. People jumped out of bed only to find the river lapping at their feet. Those who peered out of their casement windows were greeted by a surreal sight. Where there should have been land, there was now only water, and three-rigged ships wallowed on their sides where only a day before, the Quayside markets had been held. River craft had been reduced to matchwood and their remains bobbed next to great beams from the Quay and precious merchandise of all kinds. Among the debris floated the bodies of those who had died in their beds as the central arch of the bridge had collapsed, hurling them and their shops down into the surging river below.

Alerted by the ear-splitting roar accompanying the collapse of the middle section of the Bridge, several families made their way on to the parapet in stunned disbelief at what was happening. Only gradually did their own precarious situation dawn on them, as the ancient masonry groaned beneath their feet and threatened to give way at any moment.

Mr Fiddes the storekeeper led his family and servants to safety on the Gateshead side of the bridge. At this late stage his maid stammered out that she had left her bundle of possessions – probably all that she had in the world – back in the shop. She wondered if Mr Fiddes might be kind enough to return with her and collect it? The gallant Fiddes reluctantly agreed, and together they picked their way back over the crumbling bridge. Fortune does not always favour the brave, and as they sought to make their way to safety, the arch gave way beneath their feet, hurtling them both to a watery death in the foaming cauldron below.

Nearby, the Weatherley family seemed destined to share the same fate as Fiddes and his maid, as the fall of the bridge arches had isolated them and cut off any obvious escape route. Moreover, the abutment, to which they were clinging, was disintegrating under the force of the torrent. They were surely doomed.

Geordie Woodford, a local bricklayer thought otherwise. He observed that although the timber and masonry supports of the shops on the bridge had been swept away, the cantilevered extensions had remained in place, suspended out over the river. Maybe, just maybe, they might be capable of bearing the weight of a human being. Geordie decided to take the gamble. Courageously edging his way forward, he broke through partitions between the shops, until he was in reach of Mr Weatherley and his family (who had by now given up all hope of rescue and spent their time huddled in prayer). One by one, Geordie guided them to safety, with timber and masonry falling all around them. After what seemed like an eternity, Weatherley, his family and his servants, all managed to reach dry land, and brave Geordie Woodford was the toast of Tyneside.

There had been a number of remarkable escapes apart from that of the Weatherleys. The house of Patten, the general dealer, fell into the river and miraculously bobbed to the surface again, being of timber-framed construction. It remained afloat, and caught by the current, off it sailed into the night. Down the river it went, past Wallsend and Hebburn, until finally it came to rest upon the mudflats of Jarrow Slake. Would-be rescuers rushed towards it to give assistance.

On entering, they found a cat and dog waiting patiently to be fed, but otherwise none the worse for their amazing experience.

Later that day, further sections of the bridge structure collapsed into the depths of the river. Clearly there was now no question of repair, and a totally new bridge would be required. Completed in 1781, this plain Georgian structure gave way to Armstrong's famous Swing Bridge of 1873, but we would be wrong in thinking that all trace of the medieval bridge has disappeared. For in the cellars of the Watergate Building at the Newcastle side of the Swing Bridge, now a popular pub, two ribbed land arches can still be seen – all that remains of the original twelve which once graced the most important single structure in Newcastle.

Despite the scale of the catastrophe, only six people lost their lives in the Great Flood. Moreover, it ought to be borne in mind that although flooding was a constant danger, fire posed a far greater menace to life and property in a largely timber-built town. In the middle of the nineteenth century, an event occurred that was to rock Newcastle – quite literally – to its very foundations.

A Taste of Hell – The Great Fire, 6th October 1854

Surviving contemporary photographs give us a

vivid insight of the mid-nineteenth century Quayside. A jumbled mass of seventeenth century houses can be seen huddled beneath the elegant bell tower of All Saints Church, as if for protection. Many of these timber-framed houses had long since been converted into warehouses in order to service the booming local economy, but where they were still inhabited, contemporary trade directories suggest that they contained a social mix that was rare elsewhere in Victorian Britain. For in the central Quayside area, doctors, lawyers and other professionals lived cheek by jowl with publicans, labourers and artisans. The Newcastle riverside may have had aesthetic appeal, but on the Gateshead side, a series of high, fortress-like warehouses rose from the waterfront.

The highest of these buildings was known as Bertram's Warehouse, named after its builder and original owner, although it had long since been taken over by the County Fire Office. Each of its seven storeys provided convenient and apparently safe storage for large quantities of sulpha, naptha, nitrate of soda and manganese. Adjacent to this building stood Wilson's Worsted Factory. At the time of the fire, it contained sacks of wool and ominously enough, large vats of inflammable oil.

Both of these buildings backed onto the

nondescript street known as Hillgate, the south side of which comprised tall barrack-like tenements used to house unskilled workers and their families. These insanitary tenements were densely populated (in Church Walk, one attic contained ten people – and this was far from exceptional) and rose in grim tiers up to the ancient Churchyard of St Mary's.

12.30 a.m. on the 6th October, 1854, the local residents were in a state of uproar. Flames were issuing from the windows of Wilson's Factory and already licking at Bertram's Warehouse. Hundreds of people hastily pulled on clothes and positioned themselves in the churchyard for a grandstand view of the conflagration. There was a general feeling that something exciting was about to happen.

The North British Fire Brigade had been summoned, together with a fire fighting detachment from the 26th (Cameronian) Regiment under the dashing Ensign Paynter. Several local notables also joined the fight against the flames. In the searing heat of Hillgate, Mayor Haggie of Gateshead fought alongside the Director of the Newcastle Fire Office, William Woods. Bertram, the original builder of the warehouse, offered his expertise too. Meanwhile young Alex Dobson, son of the notable Tyneside architect, remembered that the tall tower of

Davidson's Mill offered a first class view of the blaze below. Joined by Davidson junior and a number of friends, Dobson took up position on the lofty bridge which joined the mill tower to the office block. Totally absorbed by the drama unfolding around them, the young men failed to realise that their own position was becoming increasingly precarious as the flames spread relentlessly down Hillgate.

For despite the efforts of the fire fighters, the warehouse caught fire, and soon a cascade of burning sulphur began to pour from the upper windows, thus forcing Ensign Paynter and his team of fifty men back into Church Walk. Meanwhile on the Newcastle side of the river, the Quayside was lined by people transfixed by the spectacle of blue flames leaping high into the sky. In order to obtain a better view, some climbed up the rigging of ships moored nearby. The atmosphere was tense with expectation, but if the brave firefighters suspected what was about to happen, they nevertheless remained steadfastly at their posts in the searing heat.

A few minutes after three o'clock there was a low, ominous rumble. It was followed by a collossal explosion that seemed to signal the end of the world. With an ear-splitting roar, a fireball rose high into the sky. It was glimpsed as far south as Northallerton and became visible to

shipping far out to sea.

Boulders, burning timbers and fiery sulphur rained down in all directions. The veteran firemen Joseph Todd and Martin Hall died horribly, trapped by debris and then inundated by a shower of burning sulphur. Ensign Paynter was crushed to death when a wall fell on him, and one of his men was impaled on the churchyard railings. Their exposed perch destroyed by the explosion, Alex Dobson and his friends were hurled into the furnace below. At the other end of the social scale, the Hillgate Lodging House and its inmates – nobody knows how many were inside at the time – simply disappeared in the all-consuming blast. Gateshead did not suffer alone, spectators on the Newcastle side of the river were showered by the cascade of death.

Burning debris came hurtling out of the night sky, setting fire to ancient houses and mowing down bystanders as if the result of an artillery barrage. In an attempt to rescue a child, one man was decapitated and his head was sent spinning into the river. To add further terror to the scene, Newcastle was plunged into darkness as all the gas lights had been extinguished by the force of the blast. Light was soon provided from another source, as the timber framed buildings fronting the river caught fire.

The authorities realised to their horror, that all available fire tenders had been directed to the Gateshead side of the river. There, they had either been damaged by the blast, or had simply disappeared along with their crews in the shattering explosion. Help had to be summoned quickly, and the authorities were forced to turn to that new-fangled device, the telegraph. Soon fire-fighting units from across the North of England were answering Newcastle's desperate pleas for help. The Shields fire boat was quickly on the scene, but it was too late to save centuries of Newcastle's history from going up in smoke. One by one the ancient chares; Grindon,

Pallister's, Peppercorn, Colvin's, Blue Anchor and Hornsby's, all fell victim to the enveloping flames. Within a matter of hours, all were reduced to smouldering debris.

Daybreak brought a scene of unimaginable desolation on both riverbanks. Scarcely a single building stood intact, and the site of the explosion was marked by a huge crater, forty feet deep. In the shattered churchyard of St Mary's, the body of seven year old Jimmy Nicholson was found beneath the monolithic boulder that flew out of the night and killed him. The remains of the firefighters were recognised from their charred clothing and personal effects. The identity of one fireman was established by virtue of the distinctive fire hose nozzle he was still holding. Similar difficulties were encountered in identifying the remains of Alex Dobson and his friends. For the authorities however, the injured presented a more pressing problem than the dead at this stage.

Hundreds of injured people needed assistance, and a casualty clearing station was established in the Fishmarket extension of the (badly damaged) Guildhall. The seriously injured were taken to the Infirmary, among them the Fire Chief Isaac Anderson, who later died of his terrible wounds.

In refreshing contrast to this sad detritus of

disaster, there had been a number of near miraculous escapes from certain death. In Oakwellgate, a couple, on hearing the explosion, leaped out of bed. Seconds later a huge boulder crashed through the roof, smashed through the bed, and disappeared through the floorboards. The couple, who were shaken but otherwise unhurt, were lucky. In Church Walk, an entire family of four, the Harts, were killed in identical circumstances. Survival was a matter of luck. Nine year old Mary Bewick died as her ramshackle tenement home collapsed on top of her, but a few yards away in Hillgate, a little girl climbed into a 'netty' or primitive earth closet, and later emerged unscathed and puzzled at the fuss being made of her.

The firefighters too had miraculous escapes. One fireman was dug out alive from debris the day following the explosion. Elsewhere, a soldier took refuge behind a wall and witnessed his colleagues perish in the explosion. Mayor Haggie had perhaps the most spectacular escape. The Mayor had been fighting the flames from an exposed forward position in Hillgate. Seeking to discover the progress being made in Church Walk, the Mayor exchanged places with Councillor Pattison of Westgate Ward. Pattison volunteered to take his place, but no sooner did Haggie reach Church Walk than the explosion took place. Haggie hurled himself under a nearby fire tender, just in time to avoid being crushed by falling timber and masonry. The tender was crushed by falling debris but a policeman pulled the Mayor to safety just in time. Recovering from his ordeal, Haggie learned that Pattison was dead, blown to oblivion in exactly the same spot where Haggie had been standing just a few minutes previously.

Surprisingly enough, the final death toll was officially no higher than fifty-three, though this figure does not include the unknown numbers who died when the Lodging House disintegrated under the blast – it seems likely that the real figure was significantly higher. Structural damage was widespread, and over eight hundred people were made homeless. Almost all of them belonged to families where the breadwinner was a casual labourer who by definition needed to live close to his place of work. The financial straits forced upon such families can easily be imagined, and a benevolent fund totalling £11,000 was collected and distributed. Although the site – stretching from the Guildhall to the Customs House, and reaching back as far as Akenside Hill – was cleared for rebuilding, the authorities decided to substitute commercial buildings for houses. John Dobson (who, it will be recalled lost his 26-year-old son Alex in the fire) designed the spacious layout of Lombard, King and Queen Streets in place of the devastated old chares.

The fire is largely forgotten now, but here and there, a few reminders can still be found. Most of those who lost their lives were interred in Jesmond Cemetery, where their Victorian sepulchural memorials are well-worth seeking out. In Gateshead itself, the crater marking the explosion has long since been filled in, but the site lies just east of the Tyne Bridge, and is now covered by Hillgate car park. Nor is there any indication that a traveller passing over Mr Stephenson's High Level Bridge at one time could have looked down upon a seething mass of humanity, for Hillgate and Oakwellgate – the scenes of such heroic sacrifice – were long ago torn down, and both are now access roads without the slightest indication of the carnage that took place there.

Yet the odd suggestion that something terrible once occurred here can still be found. The occasional vitrified stone – proof of the heat generated by the explosion – still turns up on waste ground, and from a terrace just below St Mary's Church there is a good view of the area devastated by the blast. And there, on the north wall of the church it is possible to see one of the huge boulders deposited here on that fateful

October night, when, for the people of Gateshead and Newcastle, hellfire and brimstone became a reality.

Not all accidents and disasters that have befallen Newcastle have involved either large loss of life or widespread structural damage. Some accidents – especially those involving animals, a bizarre note upon which to close this chapter.

Killer Sheep!

In 1758 a flock of sheep was being driven to slaughter in the Close, when suddenly one bolted, and the butcher's dog set off in hot pursuit. The two animals left a trail of havoc in the Sandhill Market, overturning tables and frightening shoppers. At last, the sheep ran along the Close and disappeared down a nearby chare leading to the river. The dog came bounding after it, and in a desperate bid to escape, the demented animal leapt into the Tyne. Unfortunately, two clothes dyers were at work on a scaffold directly beneath. Shocked and terrified by the sight of the sheep flying towards them, they overbalanced and fell into the river. Sad to relate, the current carried them away and they drowned before assistance could be given. The fate of the sheep is not recorded.

The Dive-Bombing Donkey of
Castle Garth

On 7th December 1733 a showman came to Newcastle and advertised himself as a 'Bird-man'. A huge crowd assembled at the Castle Garth to watch the would-be birdman glide safely to earth. Most people would have been content with this performance, but not the birdman. Egged on by the crowd, he attempted to prove that flying was easy – so easy that even a donkey could do it. The bird-man's fixed wings were attached to a donkey that had the misfortune to be standing close by. Weights were fastened to the beast's legs, and the donkey was launched from the top of the Keep. A flying donkey can only go in one direction and it fell down to earth with a crash. It was fortunate for the donkey that the crowd cushioned its fall, but many spectators were injured by the flailing legs of the animal, and a small girl is said to have died later.

These days the Castle Garth is one of the most fascinating corners of old Newcastle, and happily for the visitor, there is no hazard from low flying donkeys either.

Chapter Four

THE SUPERNATURAL

WITCHES AND WARLOCKS

It is not difficult to see why even the most ludicrous of superstitions should have held a grip over our ancestors. For most of our nation's history, only the very richest in society could afford access to doctors and, even then, most of the cures were highly dubious. The bulk of the population was forced to rely upon such relief as could be obtained from herbs, potions and general homeopathic practice. Although those who claimed to possess expert knowledge in this field, found their services in great demand, they could equally find themselves the subject of scurrilous gossip too. In the seventeenth century this could have fatal consequences for the practitioner. A woman innocently attempting to ease the sufferings of a neighbour by means of herbal remedies, might find herself arrested for witchcraft and put on trial for her life. Ironically enough, when all else seemed to be failing them, the Newcastle authorities themselves had been known to resort to magic and superstition.

For instance in 1646 the town was ravaged by yet another plague. No doubt mindful of the huge loss of life caused by the 1636 outbreak, the Corporation sent to Scotland for hire of the celebrated 'Lee Penny'. To drink water within which the 'Penny' had been immersed, was to be guaranteed immunity from plague for the rest of the drinker's life, and the Lee family made a lucrative business out of hiring the amulet out to various towns suffering from the plague. Advertising 'hype' is not a late twentieth century invention, and the 'Penny' came to Newcastle complete with a list of satisfied customers who solemnly swore that they had remained free from the plague while their sceptical neighbours had perished all around them.

Impressed with the alleged properties of the 'Penny', the Newcastle Corporation offered to buy it from the Lee family for a huge sum of money. The Lees understandably refused, and fearful of the intentions of the Newcastle civic fathers, they spirited the object back over the border again. Given that many lives were lost in the 'visitation', it was odd that the Corporation should have offered so much money for the talisman considering its obvious inefficacy. Odder still was the fact that less than three years after the town fathers had pinned their faith in magic, they should be seeking to root out and destroy the very people who were supposed to practice it.

'Thou shalt not suffer a Witch to Live'
Mid-seventeenth century Europe was gripped by witchcraft hysteria. This popular fear was closely related to the rise of the reformed

Church and its fundamentalist approach to the Bible. (Exodus XXII, V18) 'Thou shalt not suffer a witch to live' was taken quite literally.

By 1640 an alleged witch could be brought to trial by an anonymous and unsupported accusation, and the onus of proving innocence rested with the accused, who was usually some lonely old woman, guilty of nothing more sinister than of talking to a pet or of attempting to heal a sick neighbour, or the discovery of a 'witch's mark' – usually some blemish that would not bleed when pricked with a pin. Finding these marks was apparently a skilled operation, and a band of professional witch-finders soon began to roam the country in search of trade. It became something of a fashion to have a witchfinder search your town, and in 1649 the Newcastle Corporation sent for a 'Scottish expert' – almost certainly the notorious John Kincaid – to deal with the town's witch population.

On Kincaid's arrival the town bellman tramped the streets calling upon citizens to denounce their neighbourhood witch. Thirty suspects were rounded up and marched to the Guildhall for 'examination'. Once inside, they were forced to go through the indignity of being searched for likely witch marks. When one was located, Kincaid stabbed it with a (probably retractable) pin. If either the wound did not bleed, or the woman did not cry out, then guilt was proven. It was in Kincaid's interest that he should find a lot of witches in Newcastle. He was being paid 20s per conviction.

Kincaid boasted that he was so expert in his trade that he could detect a witch by sight alone, and he pointed out a particularly vicious individual to prove it. This puzzled Lt. Hobson, the honest (if dim-witted) Deputy Governor of the town, for Hobson knew the woman in question to be a decent, God-fearing soul. She was not at all the kind to take part in Satanic orgies and go around cursing people. Kincaid insisted on her guilt and proceeded to pierce a suspect mark with a pin. Sure enough, the woman seemed oblivious and the wound did not bleed. Hobson was unconvinced, he snatched the pin away from Kincaid and tried himself. This time the woman did squeal and blood spurted out. Hobson had proved beyond reasonable doubt that the woman was no witch.

It is a pity that Hobson was unable to save the lives of the fifteen other people who were found guilty of witchcraft and hanged on the Town Moor on 21st August 1650. Their bodies were cut down from the gallows and carefully interred in St Andrew's Churchyard. Evidence from the Parish Register of St Mary's Gateshead suggests that many more may have shared the

same fate. For instance we read that 6*d* was paid 'for a grave for a witch'. This was a large sum of money by contemporary standards, and it seems likely that it reflects the cost of the iron rivets that would have been driven into the knee joints of an alleged witch to prevent her walking after death.

With a question mark now hanging over his ethical practice, Kincaid left Newcastle for the promise of rich pickings in rural Northumberland. After many adventures, he fell foul of a powerful landowner and was forced to flee across the border. Nemesis eventually caught up with Kincaid, and legend has it that he himself was burnt at the stake on a charge of witchcraft. Before his death he is said to have admitted responsibility for the deaths of over 220 women. And all for the price of 20 shillings per head.

Academics now regard the witch hunts as little more than mass hysteria whipped up by the Church and prolonged by the witch finders. Others suggest that the remarkable similarities in extracted confessions from different parts of Europe, points to the existence of a genuine witch cult. Certainly in Newcastle there were people quite happy to advertise the fact that they dabbled in the occult – especially when expertise in the black arts promised lucrative rewards. The reader cannot help but wonder what those stern seventeenth century town fathers would have made of 'Black Jacky Johnson'.

Black Jacky Johnson

Novocastrians in the first quarter of the nineteenth century, on the verge of making crucial
decisions, were likely to pay a visit to Black Jacky
Johnson of Dog Bank as an extra precaution.
Jack was no mere necromancer, but a 'Professor'
of the black arts. To be specific, he was the owner
of a magic mirror that could tell the future to
whoever crossed his palm with silver.

Jack had been fortunate in acquiring a copy of
the work of celebrated Greek Magus Cornelius
Agrippa. This book contained instructions on
how to build a magic mirror, together with a
bewildering array of spells and potions, advice
on rune-casting and the art of the medium.

Black Jack specialised in revealing the identity
of future husbands to anxious ladies. Moreover,
long before Freud came upon the scene, Black
Jack had a lucrative sideline in dream interpretation, and he was equally well known for his skill
in recovering stolen goods. His magic mirror
was apparently so accurate that thieves would
return stolen property on merely learning that
their victim had gone to consult Black Jack.

Whereas Jack remained popular with the
ordinary people of Newcastle, the Corporation
disliked him and considered that he gave their

town a bad name. They persecuted Jack and eventually drove him out of the town boundaries, causing him to set up home at Byker Bar. Jack, who died in 1837, was a showman to the last. It is said that he was struck down in the act of dealing out tarot cards. He remained motionless for several days until he finally keeled over, stone dead. In spite of the persecutions of the Corporation, Jack was generous to the people of Newcastle and left them his 'kist' or coffer full of spell books and recommendations. Among them was this formula for curing acne.

It involved picking up as many sea-pebbles as the sufferer had spots. These pebbles should then be placed in a little cloth bag and left at a crossroads. Sooner or later a passer-by would see the bag and pick it up out of natural curiosity. This would be a mistake on their part, because the power of the spots had been sympathetically transferred to the pebbles, and whoever picked them up would soon find themselves suffering from acne.

Among the many spells found in Jack's kist was this one, difficult of execution and surely disappointing in terms of results:

How a Person may render Himself Invisible

Get a black cat without a white hair on its

body, boil it for three hours on a Sunday during the time of Divine Service; take out its heart and dry it in a new oven that has never been used, till you can reduce it to a fine powder to be concealed seven nights about a churchyard; to where you must repair every night at precisely 12 o'clock; on the last night you take the powder you will see another, who will walk along with you to the churchyard gates; as soon as you arrive be sure to give him the half of it, *or else you are sure of destruction:* and ever after as long as you carry any of this powder about with you, you shall be invisible.

During his lifetime (and some would say beyond it!) Jack kept company with fellow warlocks and witches. Legend has it that he used to frequent the 'Tambourine House' in Sandgate, where the local covens gathered.

The Tambourine House

The house was so-called because of the fiendish laughter and wild tambourine music often heard coming from within. In actuality the tavern was a house of ill repute, and it seems likely that the sinister associations were invented by anxious parents in the hope of deterring their offspring from venturing too near this den of vice and corruption. The tavern, which stood at the western end of St Annes Street, was demolished last century, and this is just as well as many believed that the devil himself had been in that building.

The story is told of how one night when the wind howled and there was a hunter's moon high in the sky, the Sandgate coven held an 'Esbat' – a special festival in the course of which the company summoned forth the Devil. Old Nick appeared on cue, but oddly enough he took the form of an ordinary man. This was disappointing both in itself and because he paid far more attention to the food on the table than the wild orgy unfolding around him. Even so, everyone present knew that he really was the Devil because at one in the morning he went to the centre of the floor, stood quite still and then shot off through the roof like a rocket!

In retrospect, it might have been more appropriate had he made his exit through the floorboards given the relative positions of Heaven and Hell. For decades afterwards, this part of Newcastle had a sinister reputation, and one night, a hard-pressed keelman's wife decided to turn this to her advantage in order to teach her wayward husband a lesson he would never forget.

The keelman unfailingly came home in a

drunken state every night, and totally dis-
regarded his wife's pleas to curb his excesses.
One day she had a brainwave. Mindful of the
reputation of the Tambourine Tavern, she
decided to borrow a 'Devil' fancy dress costume.
She then persuaded her brother to don it,
pretend that he was the Devil and leap out at the
keelman as he tottered home from the pub. The
brother-in-law put on the costume and took up
position in a dark entry. Sure enough, the
keelman came staggering towards him and the
'Devil' jumped out.

'Whe are ye?' asked the surprised keelman.

'Ahm the Divil. An if ye divvent mend yer
ways, aal tek ye back wi' me.' The keelman stood
amazed.

'The Divil eh? Ee whey fancy that. Shek me
hand 'cause ahm married ter yer sister!'

THINGS THAT GO BUMP
IN THE NIGHT

Since time immemorial, people have been
fascinated by the supernatural. Tales would be
swopped in the convivial atmosphere of a local
tavern. Come closing time, candles would be
snuffed, the last remaining customers would be
ejected, and as the door closed behind him, the
drinker would be left to stumble home through
the warren of dark alleys. Alone in the night,

footsteps would echo and the shadows confuse, as objects and places so familiar in daylight hours, would now take on an air of menace. The imagination could run riot as each dark entry would seem capable of harbouring all manner of indescribable terrors.

A place or a building associated with a bloody or tragic past is often claimed to be haunted. Newcastle's ancient defences have witnessed much bloodshed over the centuries, and one particular tower is said to be haunted by a last defender who steadfastly refuses to leave.

The Sallyport Cavalier

The remains of Newcastle's thirteenth century town wall are some of the best preserved in the country although large sections of it have disappeared, and the Sallyport of Carpenter's Tower is now marooned high on a hill over-looking the historic Pandon district. It has been claimed that the postern gate actually pre-dates the building of the Edwardian Walls, and it is certainly true that a great deal of Roman material was discovered during the building of nearby City Road. Much seventeenth century debris including, cannon balls, sword blades, a siege mine gallery (aligned towards the Sally-port) and human remains were also found hereabouts. Given the strategic importance of the Sallyport, and the role it played during the epic Great Siege of 1644 this evidence of violent struggle should not surprise us.

The Royalist defenders were able to defy the besieging Scots from July until October 20th 1644. At three o'clock that afternoon, the barrage lifted and the numerous subterranean mines driven deep under the town walls were fired. In a series of concerted attacks, the Scottish pikemen stormed through the result-ant breaches with 'colours flying and drums roaring'. An eyewitness supplied the following description of:

> The thousand of musket balls flying like hailstones...the clanging and carving of naked unsheathed swords; the pushing of pikes crying for blood; the carkasses of men lying like dead dogs upon the groaning street

The bloody hand-to-hand fighting continued for two hours but the situation was hopeless as the outnumbered garrison could never hope to stem the tide of pikemen surging in through the shattered walls. Many of those defending the towers fought to the death, while the remainder were pushed back street by street until they were forced to surrender. It is believed that over one thousand people perished in the assault, among them perhaps, the Sallyport Cavalier.

The Tower survived the ferocious attack of the Scots, but in the subsequent repairs and conversion into a guild meeting house, the Tower lost its martial appearance. A tiled roof capped by corner pavilions was added, and Georgian windows replaced the medieval arrow slits. Various groups started to meet there, and before long rumours began to circulate that the Tower was haunted by the ghost of a cavalier.

By all accounts he is a friendly ghost, and former caretakers have spoken of him in affectionate terms. His appearances seem to have been characterised by a tendency to make dramatic entrances. One lady stood wide eyed as a figure in seventeenth century dress suddenly rose from the floor, revolved upwards and then disappeared through the ceiling. This dramatic manifestation might be explained by the presence of a spiral staircase at this point in days gone by. The hall on the first floor is certainly atmospheric but it is many years since the phantom cavalier has been spotted. Even so, the legend persists that the fortunate few may still catch a glimpse of his figure as he stands at the Tower windows, gazing out over the town he fought and died for.

The religious houses of Newcastle may not have the violent history of the Sallyport Tower, but this has not prevented them from acquiring a number of spectral residents during the course of the centuries. St Andrew's Churchyard has a long association with the interment of witches and executed criminals. We might therefore expect the churchyard to be haunted (it is certainly a matter of conjecture as to what dreadful sight caused an eighteenth century sexton to collapse and die of fright, thus falling into a grave he had just been digging!) Surprisingly, neither witches nor felons haunt St Andrews; the only ghost in that churchyard is that of a frail, gentle girl.

The Girl in the Blue Muslin Dress

A very old story tells of how an early nineteenth century curate fell in love with, and sought to marry the daughter of a wealthy landowner who lived on the outskirts of Newcastle. The course of love did not run smoothly and the two became estranged as the result of a petty quarrel. On rethinking the situation, the young curate was determined to bring about a reconciliation. One evening when he was about to leave the church and ride over to his beloved's house in order to beg forgiveness, he caught an unexpected glimpse of the girl herself walking through the churchyard. The curate recognised her familiar features and her favourite pale blue muslin dress. Concluding that his sweetheart was as eager to effect a reconciliation as he was, he rushed out into the churchyard to greet her, only to find it deserted. Of the girl, there was not the slightest trace. Puzzled and dismayed by her disappearance, the curate rode out to her home the very next morning. On arrival he found the blinds drawn and the household plunged into mourning. He was solemnly informed that the girl had suddenly taken ill and died the previous evening. Strangely enough, she had died at exactly the moment that he spotted the figure walking in the churchyard. Even stranger was the fact that on her deathbed she had been wearing the blue muslin dress.

According to the story, her pathetic earth bound wraith flits around the gravestones at dusk in the hope of catching one last sight of her curate, but as she has not been seen for many years perhaps she has at last found peace.

Haunted Blackfriars

The Newcastle Blackfriars, now a flourishing tourist centre (and one of the best preserved medieval buildings of its kind in the country) seems always to have enjoyed the reputation of being haunted. For late at night, when the last visitor has long since left and the site is deserted, the atmosphere changes and the Phantom Friar walks abroad.

In the middle ages, two religious houses were situated on either side of Newgate Street. Whilst the grounds of the Blackfriary occupied the western side, the Convent of the Nuns of Saint Bartholomew lay on the other side of the road (on the present site of Farnon's Department Store and the Grainger Market). The legend tells of how codes of morality lapsed and 'indiscretions' took place between inhabitants of the two establishments, with the result that one of the nuns conceived a child. Ecclesiastical justice being harsh, the nun was walled up alive within the convent. The fate of the offending friar is unknown but it is said to be his ghost – a mysterious hooded figure – that is behind the disturbances at Blackfriars.

The thirteenth century layout of the Friary has been largely preserved. Visitors can browse around the workshops and watch objects being made using centuries old methods, or else dine in the hall that served as the Refectory. The craft shop lies within the western range of the Friary. In the middle ages this room was the Guest Hall and at least one king of England has rested within its walls. A peculiar chill is often noticed in this room, articles are moved overnight and found strewn about the following morning. A ghostly cowled figure has been seen to stand by a certain door, glide across the grassed-over cloisters and then vanish in the gloom. Staff have reported seeing the same unidentified hooded figure emerge from a blocked-up recess (once a fireplace) and cross the Guest Hall/craft shop only to disappear through a solid masonry wall at the opposite end of the room.

Is the Friar doomed to wander the site in penance for his sins? Or is he searching for something left here long ago? Someday charming Blackfriars will reveal its secrets, but until then, any explanation must remain speculative.

Jack the Beadle

For the prospective ghost hunter, the Quayside is the most fruitful part of old Newcastle, and long ago, Pandon mothers would warn their unruly offspring that if they did not behave, the spirit of wicked 'Jack the Beadle' would carry them off. In 1858 Newcastle was outraged by the revelation that the apparently respectable Beadle of All Saints Church had actually been plundering lead from coffins and selling it for profit. The guilty man was sentenced to eighteen months' hard labour, and local children made up the following verse:

> If ye want to rob the deed,
> Gan to Jack the Beadle;

He's the man that steals the leed,
Pop goes the weasel

Legend has it that the earth-bound spirit of the pilfering Beadle still prowls around the church-yard, lantern in hand. Certainly, when moonlight shimmers on the serried gravestones and the undergrowth rustles without apparent cause, it is not too difficult to imagine that Jack is not far away. If Jack is still around, he may keep company with another of the town's notorious characters, for the wraith of Jane Jameson is said to maintain a nocturnal vigil in the Milkmarket at the eastern end of the Quayside.

Jane Jameson's Ghost

The reader will recall that Jane was a fruitseller turned matricide, hanged in 1829. One of her favourite sites for hawking merchandise was at the water 'pant' or fountain which stood close to the present-day obelisk commemorating John Wesley. An old song tells of how she greets the passer-by with the fruitseller's call:

Fine Chenee oranges, four for a penny,
Cherry ripe cornberries, take them and try

She then pleads with the late night stroller to bring her lover, Billy Ellison to her. Given that

Jane attempted to pin the blame on Billy for her mother's murder, it is not surprising that the keelman does not make the rendezvous and Jane pleads in vain. This should not lead us to conclude that Jane's ghost is lonely for just a short distance down the Quayside, a 'silky' walks abroad.

The Quayside 'Silky'

A 'silky' is the traditional Northumbrian name for a female ghost which draws attention to its presence via the rustling of silk garments. The Broad Chare area is allegedly haunted by a muschievous silky who delights in scaring those unfortunate enough to encounter her. The origins of the silky are unclear, but the haunting may be connected with the suicide of one Martha Wilson in a Trinity House almshouse in 1817. Martha was found hanged, and because of the nature of her death (believed to be suicide) she was not buried in consecrated ground, but at a nearby crossroads instead. The circumstances of her burial may well be the reason for the haunting, at any rate, the busy housewife, the worker returning home in the dark, and above all the inebriate were all fair game for the pranks of the silky. The following tale concerns a keelman who met with her one dark night as he returned from a drinking spree.

As he made his way home along the Quayside, the keelman became aware of a female figure on the opposite side of the road who seemed to be following a course parallel to his own. On the stroke of midnight, the mysterious figure turned away and slipped into Trinity Chare. The keelman had always been sceptical over the silky tales and he concluded that he was merely witnessing one of the 'cyprian nymphs' returning home. Yet he could not help but think that there was something a little strange about this particular lady – especially in the way she appeared to glide up the Chare as opposed to walk up it. Half curious, half afraid, the inebriate keelman pursued the figure. As if aware that she was being followed, the woman paused, turned, and lifting her veil beckoned towards the faltering keelman. The keelman warily approached, and to his abject horror realised that there was no head beneath the veil. Frightened out of his wits, he turned and ran down the Chare, leaving the alley echoing to shrieks of unearthly laughter.

Following his late-night encounter with 'Lady Silk' it is said that the once wayward keelman remained teetotal for the remainder of his days.

In the middle ages the Close was the most prestigious street in Newcastle. Originally a strip of land recovered from the Tyne, from the

thirteenth century onwards, aristocrats and merchants began to build town houses on either side of it. The lower storeys of the Cooperage date from this period, and it seems that with the exception of the Castle Keep, the Cooperage is the oldest secular building in Newcastle. Now a popular pub, the Cooperage appears to attract a number of spectral regulars too.

The Cooperage

In its present state, the Cooperage consists of two parts, the older of which dates back to the thirteenth century. The timber framing masks a series of beamed rooms within, one of which is the restaurant.

This room is perfectly charming when bustling with people, but when the premises are deserted, the ambiance changes and the unseen inhabitants take over. The people who work in the building are in no way subject to flights of fancy, yet a number of them have experienced weird and inexplicable phenomena. One particularly level-headed gentleman had a very unnerving encounter in the restaurant at the dead of night when the building was deserted.

Busy with some task, he became increasingly aware of being watched, yet he well knew he was totally alone. As he continued with his work, the suspicion grew that perhaps someone had slipped into the Cooperage without being seen, for the gentleman could not rid himself of the sensation that someone else was present. In order to satisfy his frayed nerves, he decided to check the restaurant just in case an intruder had broken in. As he turned he became aware of an object where no object should be. For there hovering just a few feet away from him was what could only be described as an amorphous cloud-like form – rather like cigar smoke – but with a much greater density. Unable to either move or to accept the evidence of his own eyes, he stood momentarily transfixed with shock. As soon as the power returned to his limbs, he raced down the stairs and out through the door as fast as he possibly could. Even now, although he would not readily admit to belief in the supernatural, he freely confesses that he is at a loss to explain his chilling encounter in the restaurant.

Others have witnessed paranormal pheno- mena in the restaurant area. One day, a waiter glanced up to see a long haired girl in odd- looking clothes gazing wistfully back at him for a few seconds before vanishing before his eyes. This figure has often been seen, and some staff have become so accustomed to her appearances that they merely ignore her and continue with their work. On one occasion a girl was seen to enter the ladies' toilets just before closing time.

As she failed to emerge, staff anxiously investigated only to find the room in question deserted. The only means of entry or exit was through the one door they had used.

From time to time, the upper floors echo to the sound of heavy footsteps followed by the slamming of doors, and whatever causes these disturbances might also be responsible for the terrifying ordeal suffered by a young cleaner in the Discotheque room.

While her colleagues worked elsewhere, the girl in question was left alone in the empty rrom. Suddenly her fellow employees heard a piercing scream and ran to the girl's assistance, but found her in a state of shock. Later, when she had calmed down sufficiently she explained what had happened. She had been busy when she glimpsed a movement out of the corner of her eye. Raising her head, she watched horrified as a luminous cloud began to materialise at the far side of the room. Paralysed with fear, she saw the unmistakable form of an arm and a fist develop within the cloud. To her abject terror, the apparition slowly but surely began to move towards her. At this point, fear overwhelmed her and she began to scream hysterically. The others rushed in, and the apparition dissolved.

Members of staff are convinced that they share the building with others unseen who, from time to time make their presence felt. Despite the cleaner's terrifying experience, few believe the ghosts to be malevolent. Spectral chuckling coupled with numerous sightings of an elderly man (who doffs his cap to ladies) has convinced them that these particular spooks are amiable enough.

What a wonderful place the Cooperage is for those who love mysteries! There again, what a wonderful old town Newcastle is for those who enjoy good, dark tales!